MW01221965

Comments on other *Amazing Stories* from readers & reviewers

"*Tightly written volumes filled with lots of wit and humour about famous and infamous Canadians.*"
Eric Shackleton, *The Globe and Mail*

"*The heightened sense of drama and intrigue, combined with a good dose of human interest is what sets* Amazing Stories *apart.*"
Pamela Klaffke, *Calgary Herald*

"*This is popular history as it should be... For this price, buy two and give one to a friend.*"
Terry Cook, a reader from Ottawa, on **Rebel Women**

"*Glasner creates the moment of the explosion itself in graphic detail...she builds detail upon gruesome detail to create a convincingly authentic picture.*"
Peggy McKinnon, *The Sunday Herald*, on **The Halifax Explosion**

"*It was wonderful...I found I could not put it down. I was sorry when it was completed.*"
Dorothy F. from Manitoba on **Marie-Anne Lagimodière**

"*Stories are rich in description, and bristle with a clever, stylish realness.*"
Mark Weber, *Central Alberta Advisor*, on **Ghost Town Stories II**

"*A compelling read. Bertin...has selected only the most intriguing tales, which she narrates with a wealth of detail.*"
Joyce Glasner, *New Brunswick Reader*, on **Strange Events**

"*The resulting book is one readers will want to share with all the women in their lives.*"
Lynn Martel, *Rocky Mountain Outlook*, on **Women Explorers**

OTTAWA TITANS

OTTAWA TITANS

Fortune and Fame in the
Early Days of Canada's Capital

HISTORY/BUSINESS
by L.D. Cross

PUBLISHED BY ALTITUDE PUBLISHING CANADA LTD.
1500 Railway Avenue, Canmore, Alberta T1W 1P6
www.altitudepublishing.com
1-800-957-6888

Copyright 2004 © L.D. Cross
All rights reserved
First published 2004

Extreme care has been taken to ensure that all information presented in
this book is accurate and up to date. Neither the author nor the
publisher can be held responsible for any errors.

Publisher	Stephen Hutchings
Associate Publisher	Kara Turner
Series Editor	Jill Foran
Editor	Dianne Smyth
Digital Photo Colouring	Scott Manktelow

We acknowledge the financial support of the Government
of Canada through the Book Publishing Industry Development
Program (BPIDP) for our publishing activities.

Altitude GreenTree Program
Altitude Publishing will plant twice as many trees as were used
in the manufacturing of this product.

National Library of Canada Cataloguing in Publication Data

CIP Data for this title is available on request from the Publisher.
Fax (403) 678-6951 for the attention of the Publishing Records Department.

ISBN 1-55153-960-8

An application for the trademark for Amazing Stories™
has been made and the registered trademark is pending.

Printed and bound in Canada by Friesens
2 4 6 8 9 7 5 3 1

Cover: Timber slide on the Ottawa River, looking towards Parliament Hill, circa 1880
(Photo reproduced courtesy of the National Archives of Canada)

Contents

Prologue 9

Chapter 1 Philemon Wright (1760 – 1839) 11

Chapter 2 Lieutenant-Colonel John By (1779 – 1836) 29

Chapter 3 Thomas MacKay (1772 – 1855) 50

Chapter 4 Nicholas Sparks (1792 – 1862) 62

Chapter 5 John Egan (1811 – 1857) 72

Chapter 6 J.R. Booth (1827 – 1925) 84

Chapter 7 E.B. Eddy (1827 – 1906) 105

Chapter 8 Thomas Ahearn (1855 – 1938) 117

Epilogue 131

Bibliography 133

Prologue

It was 10:30 a.m. when a small chimney fire started in a wooden building in Hull, across the river from Ottawa. At first the fire was considered nothing out of the ordinary. It seemed there were always fires in the shabby housing of the mill hands. Even the mills had fires from time to time. Wood was a cheap and plentiful building material, so fire prevention was not a big concern. Why, just four months earlier Hull City Council had refused to spend $1000 to buy new fire-fighting equipment because of a budget deficit.

But that morning, everything would change. A steady wind picked up, blowing from the south towards Ottawa. Soon the wind speed reached 50 kilometres an hour. The fire spread from house to house, to offices, and to factories. Then it reached the banks of the Ottawa River, where thousands of metres of dried wood were piled, waiting to be shipped to market.

Some people, seeking refuge from their burning homes and businesses, jumped in the river to escape the smoke and flames. But the water was turning warm from the heat as flaming piles of timber floated downstream.

Suddenly — spurred on by the wind and the rising flames — the fire leaped over the river. In no time, the palatial houses that the lumber barons had built beside the Chaudière Falls were gone, just like those of their mill workers. By nightfall, the Ottawa River glowed red with the reflected light of the fire. With more fuel and a strong wind, the fire slashed right through west Ottawa to Dow's Lake and the Dominion Experimental Farm. It could not be stopped. And it was spreading faster than a man could run.

Days later, when it was all over, only a few brick chimneys, blackened stone walls, and charred tree trunks remained standing. Rows of metal wheels from destroyed railway cars curved through the flattened lumberyards. Reconstruction began immediately and, 10 months later, most of the businesses and some 750 houses had been rebuilt — out of wood.

The Great Fire of 1900 marked the end of the capital as a lumber city. In the 20th century, Ottawa would become a government city. And now, in the 21st century, it is becoming a city of technology.

But lumber was where it began.

Chapter 1
Philemon Wright
(1760 – 1839)

*"It may [be] to your interests to keep the Grand River
from becoming settled, but you may bet your best
beaver skin on this, that there is at least five
hundred thousand acres of uncleared land fit
for cultivation on the banks."*

Philemon Wright, in his address to prominent
members of the Montreal fur trading companies,
whose report stated there was not 500 acres of
arable land along the whole river.

he dense bush north of Montreal had not
been well explored by the time Philemon
Wright came upon it. In fact, only Native
hunters and fur traders were familiar with the uninhabited
country. Nobody in Montreal knew or cared about the area,
and settling it was the last thing on anybody's mind. Except
Philemon Wright's.

A gentleman farmer from Woburn, Massachusetts, Wright travelled north to Montreal every fall in search of a better market for his farm produce. It was on one of these trips, in 1796, that he undertook a journey of exploration up the Ottawa River (then called the Grand River). At first he passed a few small settlements, but as he continued, signs of civilization were scarce. By the time he had reached 130 kilometres out, the land seemed both majestic and unoccupied.

What impressed Wright most during his journey were the extensive stands of fine timber that he saw along the Upper Ottawa River. The thought of all those trees stayed with him. A year later he made a return visit, exploring the country and the Crown lands available on both sides of the St. Lawrence River. His route extended from Quebec City to Montreal then back up the Ottawa River as far as the Chaudière Falls. Still, he did nothing.

A third visit followed in 1798. It was during this visit that Wright realized a settlement around the Chaudière Falls area offered not only a wealth of land, but future prosperity for anyone willing to move there. Back home in Woburn, he accepted an offer from John Fassett of Burlington, Vermont, to buy a half-interest in a Warrant of Survey. This warrant deemed the holder eligible for a substantial land grant from the British Crown if he surveyed the land, cleared it, and brought in settlers. One of the parcels of land covered by the warrant was around the Chaudière Falls. But, not surprisingly, Wright failed to convince any of his American neighbours that it was a good idea to leave their cleared farms and start again in the wilderness on a promised grant of land from the British Crown.

Warrants of Survey were only issued to "men of substance" who were deemed to be loyal to the Crown. As it turned out, John Fassett did not meet the criteria. When the government of Lower Canada discovered that Fassett was not only a Yankee rebel, but also a land speculator who had no interest in developing lands in Canada, his warrant was cancelled. Meanwhile, the fur trading companies were making it very clear that they did not want any settlers in their fur trading areas. Most men would have given up at this point — but not Wright.

Philemon Wright was the fifth child and youngest son of farmer Thomas Wright and his wife Elizabeth Chandler. In 1782, he married Abigail Wyman, and they went on to have seven children. Described as a tall man with a strong, broad build, Wright had flaxen hair that was brushed straight back, a high forehead, thick brows, and penetrating observant eyes. He was the owner of considerable property around Woburn.

Before learning of Fassett's cancelled warrant, Wright had asked two "respectable men" from his Woburn neighbourhood to accompany him to the Chaudière Falls area the following summer, examine the situation for themselves, and objectively report back to their neighbours on what they saw. Their report, which was later published in *Canadian Magazine* in 1824, said, in part, "We climbed to the top of one hundred or more trees to view the situation of the country ... By the timber we could judge the nature of the soil, which we found to answer our expectations. Having examined well the nature of the township, we descended the river and arrived, after much fatigue, at Montreal."

One advantage of the dense timber growth was that it made it easy to climb lookout trees to view the lay of the land. The technique involved chopping down a small tree so its branches became entangled with those of a larger tree, then scrambling up the incline, which formed a convenient ladder to the top.

The three men evaluated the richness of the earth and the quantity of timber and mapped out the main topographical features of the land. It was on the return trip back through Montreal that Wright learned that Fassett's warrant was invalid. It was a severe blow, but he was able to convince the land agent of his own integrity. He received verbal assurances that the Crown would look favourably on his application for a warrant in his own name. Wright immediately made a formal request and returned home with a positive report.

The people of Woburn were considerably more impressed by this new report. And, in 1800, 40-year-old Wright was finally able to convince a group of his neighbours to accompany him to the dense bush north of Montreal. In March of that year, Wright, along with 37 men, 5 women, and 21 children, set off on the 800-kilometre journey to the Chaudière Falls. The brave band of New Englanders brought with them 14 horses, 8 oxen, and 7 sleighs loaded with mill equipment, agricultural implements, carpentry tools, house-hold effects, and provisions for the trip. They reached Montreal in just nine days time, but progress up the north shore of the Ottawa River was considerably slower — the runners on their sleighs were wider than the local variety and, as a result, the group could only use part of the existing trail. They managed to cover only 24 kilometres a day. Then, 130 kilometres from their destination, the road ended completely.

Years later, while relating the group's experiences to the House of Assembly (where he was a member), Wright recalled, "Before night came, we cleared away the snow and cut down trees for fire, the women and children sleeping in covered sleighs, the men with blankets around the fire and the cattle made fast to the standing trees ... We proceeded on for three or four days then we travelled upon the ice until we reached our destination. My guide was unacquainted with the ice, as our former journeys were by water. We went very slowly lest we might lose our cattle, keeping the axemen forward trying every rod of the ice, which was covered with snow."

After six more days, the Chaudière Falls were in sight. But soon another problem confronted the party: though they had arrived safely at the falls, they had to climb up from the river's edge onto the highland. Everyone lent a hand cutting through the thick brush while climbing, pulling, and shoving all their possessions about six metres straight up the bluff from the river.

Once on top, they could see magnificent forests as far as the horizon, sparkling water in the river below, and the white foam and spray from the rapids beside them. The Natives called the Chaudière Falls *Asticou,* which means "kettle" or "cauldron." And it was here that the New Englanders founded Wright's Town, which also became known as Wrightville. Later it was called Hull, and it is currently known as Gatineau. On the opposite shore were the stands of pine and cedar and the cliffs from which, 60 years later, the first Parliament Buildings rose in a settlement called Bytown (now Ottawa).

That first year, the woods rang from sunrise to sunset with the sounds of axes hitting wood and tall trees hitting the ground. Wright later described this early period to the circle of Assembly members: "As soon as we began our cutting and clearing work, the Chiefs of two tribes came to us and looked over all our tools with astonishment. While we had brought only the most essential items with us on the long trip, they had never seen such an assortment of implements and asked by signs and gestures what each was used for. We demonstrated for them how our saws, axes, hammers and chisels worked."

Word spread quickly. Day after day, more Natives showed up to watch the first settlers near the Chaudière Falls clear the land with their strange tools and techniques and their fascinating draft animals. Obviously the settlers were not considered a threat because some of the Natives brought their children along with them to follow the activity and touch the tame animals. Tentative hands reached out and, when not rebuffed, patted and stroked the huge beasts.

"We could not talk each other's language at that time," recalled Wright, "but they indicated that they would like to try cutting down trees with one or two of our axes.

Their hatchets were small and light while our axes weighed from four to five pounds. We showed them how to balance themselves firmly before swinging the axes. They caught on fast and, being in excellent physical condition, were able to accomplish the task in no time."

For about 10 days, a procession of Native visitors came and went from the little settlement, showing up in the early morning and leaving before sunset. These visits often included exchanges of small presents between the two groups. Some of the settlers' pots and cooking utensils were readily traded for food items like maple syrup and venison, which were a welcome addition to their diet. It was a barter between equals, and each side felt they had made a good deal.

"One day we saw a man and his wife pulling a small child on a bark sleigh," Wright said to the House of Assembly. "They stopped near our bush-clearing work and pointed in some alarm to the ice on the nearby river where we had been walking and drawing logs. It became clear to us that they felt there was some danger in what we were doing … The man showed us how to test the ice with each step, clearing off the

Portrait of Philemon Wright, circa 1800 – 1810, by an unknown artist.

snow, checking the colour and using his small hatchet to make sure of its firmness. We were most appreciative of his instruction. He had most probably saved our lives and our new settlement. We never saw him or his family again but every year when the water froze over we remembered his advice."

In summing up his account, Wright said, "I must acknowledge that I was never acquainted with any people that more strictly regarded justice and equity than those people have for these past 20 years." But Wright gave no thought to what the Natives who visited his little band of pioneers would do once he had cleared their forest for his lumber mills and farms.

Initially, Wright and his settlers were called "Yankee squatters," even though they had Crown permission to settle there. But, as the forest was transformed into a commercial and agricultural centre, Wright came to be called the Father of the Ottawa, and the White Chief of the Ottawa. In later years, people often referred to him simply as the Squire.

Before the end of their first year near the Chaudière Falls, the settlers had cleared some land and harvested a crop of potatoes. In 1801, as part of the agreement he had with his workers, Wright took them back to Woburn and paid them their wages. By then, most of the settlers had decided they liked the freedom and challenge of their new life up the Ottawa River. So, by mutual agreement, they identified the sections of land they wanted, settled their affairs in Woburn, and came back up the Ottawa River the following year.

Wright and a crew of 10 men set about surveying the entire township. When they finished, they had hammered in 377 stakes and surveyed a total of 82,429 acres. The survey met the final requirement for Wright's application of a grant of land in his own name from the Crown. The governor gave him and his settlers 12,000 acres of the township. By previous agreement, the settlers ceded five-sixths of their land back to Wright. At the time, this was considered a reasonable fee for a promoter's services in surveying and arranging the land grant.

Moving from cutting down trees to tilling the ground, Wright had 800 acres of cleared land divided into fields for different crops and animals by 1814. He had numerous settlers working on these lands, as well as on the roads connecting them, while others cleared new parcels of land. The community grew, and by 1820, over half the male population in the area was working for the Wright family. Wright himself held personal title to 12,145 acres.

By this time, Wright was growing tired of the long trips to Montreal to get supplies. He wanted basic services to be available closer to home. So, he established a blacksmith shop, a tailor shop, a shoemaker shop, a leather tannery, and a large bakehouse in Wright's Town. As well as reducing the number of supply trips, these enterprises provided employment to an even greater number of local settlers.

Ever the entrepreneur, Wright also thought better use

could be made of the trees in the land-clearing process. Soon, trees not used for building or heating the community were tied up into rafts of square-cut timber and sent downriver to sell in the open markets of Montreal and Quebec City. Merchants there paid good money for wood to be used in shipbuilding and construction. Thus began the lumber industry of the Ottawa Valley.

Wright established a small sawmill at the Chaudière Falls, and Wright's Town survived and thrived, thanks to the lucrative timber trade and the ever-growing demand for wood products in Europe and the United States.

With his town expanding and his farms producing enough food to feed everyone, Wright decided to focus even more of his attention on the timber all around him. He determined to get directly involved in selling and delivering the product to market. On one trip, he and four men, including one of his sons, decided to float a large raft of timbers down the Ottawa River to Montreal all by themselves. Their objective was to sell everything in the Port of Quebec, from where it would be shipped to England. It sounded a lot easier than it was.

Wright and his men left Wright's Town in the spring of 1806 with some 700 logs and 9000 boards tied into a makeshift raft, and 6000 oak staves hammered together. The men bobbed down the Ottawa on their clumsy raft until they reached the beginning of the Long Sault Rapids. There, Wright engaged some local Natives to help him dismantle the raft into smaller "cribs," which contained 35 logs overlaid with boards and staves. Guiding the cribs individually through the rapids was dangerous and discouraging work. Many of the cribs broke into pieces when the strong current smashed them against the rocks. Some ran aground on the shore while others were swept away, never to be seen again. The group wasted valuable time gathering up all the wood scattered along the shoreline.

When a logjam occurred, the men had to wade into the waist-deep cold swirling water and pry the logs loose with iron-tipped pike poles. Finally, after 36 days, they cleared the rapids, reassembled the raft, and floated on downstream towards their market. To avoid the Lachine Rapids, Wright took his raft around the north shore of the Island of Montreal and then into the St. Lawrence River. Because of the beating the raft had sustained on its journey, it broke apart several times on the way from Montreal to Quebec City and had to be hammered back together again. This caused further delays.

It took Wright and his men over two months to reach Quebec City, and when they finally got there (in August), bad news awaited them. The sale had fallen through due to their late delivery. Not only could Wright not sell his staves, the timber market was in decline and there were no buyers for his logs and boards. His 64-day journey, which was heralded the beginning of the lumber trade in the Ottawa Valley, appeared to have been in vain.

Wright had no option but to wait in Quebec, hoping

that the market would improve and that a buyer would appear. Three months later, in November, some British "timber droghers" sailed into port and he was able to sell them his raft. Their arrival gave credence to rumours that the British Navy and its purchasing agents were short of supplies. Wright was not aware that Napoleon was sealing off the Baltic ports, depriving Britain of its traditional source of timber. But he did know that there would be a good market for oak staves and mast timbers of white pine. The navy's specifications of a minimum length of 112 feet and a butt width of 40 inches were not a problem. The Ottawa Valley was full of giant white pines.

Encouraged by the possibility of an eventual good outcome, Wright determined to make more profitable lumber raft runs down the Ottawa River. He knew he had gained valuable experience on his first run through the Long Sault Rapids, and he felt confident his next trip would not take so long. That winter, Wright sent most of his labourers into the bush to cut down timber. The sawmill ran constantly, surrounded by stacks of lumber. By the time the spring ice melted, a boom of mast timbers was anchored on the river. Squire Wright could hardly wait to start bargaining with the British Navy purchasing agents. But that May, his dreams literally went up in smoke.

Fire destroyed his mills, including the grist mill and all the sawn lumber. Not one board, nor one sack of flour, remained in the settlement. And, because he had no insurance, Philemon Wright was bankrupt. Had it not been for his sons, he would have given up. They urged him to rebuild with the proceeds from the timber still floating untouched in the river. He agreed, and took the raft safely down to Quebec. While he was gone, his men went to work. By that fall, Wright's Town had a new sawmill and a new grist mill. They still had to buy winter provisions in Montreal, but the community had survived its greatest threat to date.

The Wrights were an enterprising family in areas outside of the timber trade as well. Wright and his sons established the Hull Mining Company, a cement manufacturing facility, and also operated the first steamboat on the Ottawa River. This steamboat, called the *Union of the Ottawa*, operated between Wright's settlement and the Town of Grenville, which was south, towards Montreal. It carried both cabin and deck passengers, as well as cargoes of produce and merchandise. By 1823, Wright's Town boasted even more public amenities, including two distilleries, a hotel, a post office, a school, a brickyard, and a church with a 37-metre steeple.

As well as hard work and determination, luck played a part in Wright's success. Lieutenant-Colonel By arrived near the Chaudière Falls in 1826. The lieutenant-colonel had been commissioned by the British Government to supervise construction of the Rideau Canal. The waterway was to run from the Ottawa River south to Kingston, providing Montreal with a longer but more secure wartime supply route away from the American border. Wright was an early advocate of the canal, believing that it would facilitate commercial development of the area. Using his detailed knowledge of the region, Wright promptly offered advice and assistance to By and his Royal Engineers. Soon, his town became the major supply point for the canal builders

Wright also contracted to do some of the work. He undertook to build a dike across Dow's Swamp, which was located near the canal route, thus draining the marshy land and creating what is now Dow's Lake. Unfortunately, the canal contracts were one of the few instances where he lost money. One of his business associates had warned him at the time to "be very careful in all your transactions with Colonel By, otherwise you may be ruined." Wright wasn't ruined. But his dealings with the wily lieutenant-colonel were one instance where he did not make a profit on a business deal.

However, By did recognize the importance of the lumber trade to the development of the area and ordered a rafting channel dug on the side of the Chaudière Falls. At less than half a kilometre in length, it was an improvement over several days of hauling heavy timber overland or dismantling and reassembling log rafts to get them past the rapids. But the channel was narrow and only individual logs could pass.

In 1829, after returning from a trip to Scandinavia where he learned new lumbering techniques, Wright's son Ruggles built the first timber slide on the Ottawa River. It was a much wider channel (eight metres on the north side of the falls) that would allow the large timber rafts to pass.

Previously, much valuable timber had been badly damaged when slammed up against the large rocks by the fast-moving water. The slide was made available for the use of other lumber companies by way of a toll fee to the Wrights.

John MacTaggart, who worked on the Rideau Canal for Lieutenant-Colonel By between 1826 and 1828, was one of many people impressed with the Squire's abilities in reclaiming land and turning wild forest into productive acreage. He described Wright as "a man with a wonderful strange, quick, reflective, wild eye … [He talks] of schemes of the wildest enterprise, and he is in his glory … It was he who first proposed the Rideau Canal and I have heard him with pleasure propose other works equally great and ingenious."

When he was in his late sixties, Wright started out on yet another career. He was elected to the House of Assembly for Lower Canada and spent much of his time lobbying for the construction of public buildings in his settlement. Public buildings would give added prestige to Wright's Town, and the cost of putting them up would be borne by the Crown, not by the Squire or his residents. Who could ask for a better deal? Wright succeeded in getting a courthouse and jail for his constituents before he retired. He then turned much of the farming operation and timber business over to his sons. By that time, his holdings totalled some 37,000 acres, served by a bustling town and a brand new canal.

Wright was a hard-working man with Yankee ingenuity. While in his personal life he might not have chosen the easy route, he was always able to see the appeal of an "easy way" for others. His settlement at the site on the Ottawa River near the Chaudière Falls was a major portage and resting place on the inland water route between Montreal and Georgian Bay. To enlarge his settlement and increase its self-sufficiency, Philemon Wright often travelled abroad to convince more people to join Wright's Town. On a trip to England, where he travelled to buy purebred Devon and Hereford cattle to improve his herds, he signed up some impoverished farm hands and paid their passage in return for their labour on his land. This was common practice at the time, resulting in people starting a new life (and for many a better life) in the New World.

When he was away on his many trips, Wright wrote frequently, and at length, to his wife Abigail and his adult sons, Tiberius and Ruggles. His letters demonstrate a paternalistic concern for their welfare and that of the settlers around the Chaudière Falls. In 1820, Wright was forced to stay in Quebec City for some time to settle a land issue. He wrote home about the distilling business, gave instructions regarding his agriculture and cattle concerns, and sent his good wishes for those in the community.

By the 1820s, Wright's Town was a well-established community of some 700 people who were either transplanted New Englanders or first-generation Canadians from Europe. Wright lived in a splendid house surrounded by 800 acres of productive farmland. As for livestock, there were 123 horses,

418 oxen, 503 cows, 505 pigs, and 558 sheep.

Wright had always involved himself in every aspect of the development of his community. He shaped the early Ottawa-Gatineau region to match his own ideas and interests as well as the common good of his community and his adopted country.

The Squire died on June 3, 1839, and his remains lie in St. James Cemetery on Aylmer Road in Gatineau. His name is still prominent today.

Philemon Wright was more than an explorer and colonist. He and those who followed set the stage for the lumbering industry of the Ottawa Valley and the establishment of a settlement that would expand into the present National Capital Region. Wright was to the north shore of the Grand River (Ottawa River) what Lieutenant-Colonel By would be to the south shore. By, who had established Bytown as the main service centre during the building of the Rideau Canal, would lay the foundations for Canada's capital city.

Chapter 2
Lieutenant-Colonel John By
(1779 – 1836)

"[Lieutenant-Colonel John By has demonstrated]
a moral courage and undaunted spirit and
combination of science and management equally
exciting our admiration and deserving our praise."
Montreal Committee of Trade address to John By

J ohn By broke with family tradition. Though he had come from a long line of Thames River watermen, a profession that also included attending to customs duties, young John decided to enter the Royal Military Academy in England. He soon received a commission in the Royal Artillery then transferred to the Royal Engineers. In 1802, as a young officer, he was sent to "the Canadas" to work on the defences at Quebec City.

During this posting, By built an impressive scale model of Quebec City, which included the Plains of Abraham.

When By was recalled to fight in the Peninsular War of 1810 to 1813 against France and Spain, he took the model home with him to England (in 18 large crates) in order to plan new fortifications for the city. In the field, he served briefly under the Duke of Wellington, who was later to gain fame at the Battle of Waterloo (1815) against Napoleon. After the war, By returned to England, where he was appointed engineer officer for the Royal Gunpowder Mills. However, munitions requirements were minimal after Waterloo and he was retired on half-pay.

By was then called back to active service to construct the Rideau Canal near Montreal in Lower Canada. The canal was intended as an alternative military route linking the Grand River to the City of Kingston on Lake Ontario. It was the assignment of a lifetime. It would make or break his reputation.

Lieutenant-Colonel John By of the Royal Engineers arrived back in Canada in 1826 and left in 1832 with the Rideau Canal complete and operating. During this time, he built barracks for his troops on a hill overlooking the Ottawa River, laid out a street grid for a townsite (where his workers could live), and built a bridge over the Chaudière Falls. He also set out with his men to survey a 200-kilometre route to Kingston using an old voyageur trail. He wasted no time in building a secure navigable waterway, utilizing a natural

Lieutenant-Colonel John By directing the
building of the Rideau Canal, circa 1886.

series of inland lakes and rivers.

The reason for this waterway arose from the War of 1812, in which the United States Congress declared war on Great Britain. There was a distinct possibility that British North America (Canada) would be invaded by the United States. The conflict ended in a stalemate. The situation should never have resulted in a Declaration of War in the first

place, as the British had ordered the contentious fortifications removed two days before the United States took action.
But news travelled slowly back then and a series of military
skirmishes took place before things got straightened out.
Besides, the United States had a ten-to-one population
advantage over British North America. The U.S. had the
ability to put warships on the Great Lakes to blockade the
colony. Thus, the British decided to take defensive measures.

The Duke of Wellington, then the British master-general
of ordinance, laid out the defence strategy for Upper Canada
(Ontario) using a series of forts, loyalist settlements, and
waterways. He was an advocate for construction of the
Rideau Canal and, knowing John By's work, had recommended him for the job. The duke knew that, in addition to exem-
plary engineering skills, the man for the job had to have
excellent health and immense determination. In Wellington's
opinion, that man was John By. The lieutenant-colonel was
described by one of his associates as "a man who encountered all privations with wonderful patience and good
humour. He could sleep soundly anywhere and eat anything,
even raw pork."

So, between 1826 and 1832, an old Native canoe trail
was transformed from wilderness into a navigable waterway
providing the British Army with a safe supply route for its
inland garrisons. The St. Lawrence route was more direct, but
it was exposed to possible attack by U.S. military ships. At the
time, the demand for improved transportation systems, such

as canals and railways, emphasized the importance of the engineering profession. For centuries, the term "engineer" had meant a military man responsible for building defensive fortifications, roads, and equipment for waging war. Later, as settlements increased, more and more engineering tasks became civil or non-military.

The personal life of the man who built the Rideau Canal remains much of a mystery. While By wrote extensive professional documents to contractors with specific engineering directives, he wrote few personal letters. Even fewer survive. His inner thoughts and feelings are virtually unknown. By's wife and daughters came with him while the canal was being constructed and lived in the Bytown house he had built for them. So there were no wistful letters sent back home. Indeed, the man who built the most enduring waterway in central Canada remains an enigma. After his death, his wife Esther was less than forthcoming with her husband's papers in light of the poor treatment handed out to him by the British Government (during and after the completion of the canal). Since she died only two years after him, documents and family papers became the property of their son-in-law, Percy Ashburnham. Disinterest or carelessness may have caused them to be discarded or destroyed. Consequently, John By has, over time, become a construction of what others said about him.

William Lett, a boy in Bytown at the time of the canal construction, later became the first city clerk of Ottawa. In recalling his impressions of the appearance and personality of John By, he wrote: "Colonel By was what a physiognomist would call a 'man with a presence.' He was about five-feet-nine-inches tall, stoutly built, almost corpulent, and quite military looking. His hair was dark, complexion rather florid, and altogether he was rather jovial and good natured in looks. He was a man of great energy and determination."

Like many British officers of the time who wanted to get ahead, By may have belonged to the Order of Freemasonry. The Order was a charitable and benevolent fraternity of men bound together by vows of morality in public and private life, free public education, and freedom of religious and political views. Philemon Wright was a prominent Freemason, and Freemasonry was popular in Wright's Town at the time. As the commanding royal engineer, By presided over the official ceremony to lay the cornerstone of the canal at the flight of locks up from the Ottawa River at Bytown. It is reported that this ceremony was held "with full Masonic honours." There is no indication of what those honours might have been.

On hand for the occasion was Sir John Franklin, the naval officer and Arctic explorer who was passing down the Ottawa River at the time. Franklin, also a Freemason, was invited to place the symbolic cornerstone with Lord Dalhousie, the governor-in-chief (another Freemason). Entrance Bay (then known as Sleigh Bay) was chosen for the start of the canal because of its strategic location between two high bluffs. Another factor for the choice was the rising cost of land along the originally designated canal route. As land speculators bought up parcels of land in hopes of making a speedy profit, British officials had difficulty acquiring rights-of-way at reasonable prices.

Captain John Le Breton had hastily purchased land at Richmond Landing, a short distance away from Entrance Bay, for £499 and offered it for sale at £3000 — so that location was ruled out as a possible site for the locks in Bytown. Under the terms of the Rideau Canal Act, Lieutenant-Colonel By obtained land from Nicholas Sparks. Concerned about being able to defend the canal project, By saw the land as useful for military purposes. In a few years it became obvious that the land would not be needed and it was subdivided for civil use. Sparks was furious. Lengthy legal manoeuvring continued for years based on the contention that the Act permitted expropriation for canal construction only. Eventually, the land was returned to the Sparks Estate and has since become the commercial centre of downtown Ottawa.

The Government of Upper Canada in York (now Toronto) had commissioned a detailed survey and cost analysis of improving the internal navigation of the entire area. Its 1824 report ranged from a low estimate of £62,258 to a high of £230,785. This included a system with locks 100 feet by 22 feet. That low estimate would cause By a lot of problems when he actually built the Rideau Canal.

The canal was designed and built under By's direct supervision. Thousands of Irish and French labourers,

Scottish stonemasons, and British sappers (soldiers with the rank of private in regiments of engineers) and miners worked on the project. They battled early 19th century working conditions — as well as harsh weather and illness — to complete the entire system in just under six years. The construction of the canal was an adventure in engineering. Built by soldiers, independent contractors, and immigrant labourers through the swamps, rivers, forests, and rocks of the Canadian Shield, it tied together the pioneer communities that developed along its length.

Working conditions during the canal's construction were primitive. Almost all the work was done with hand tools, gunpowder, and oxen. In addition to the hard physical labour, canal workers had to contend with mosquitoes, black-flies, dysentery, cholera, and malaria (also called ague or swamp fever). As they slogged through thick bogs and heavily forested riverbanks, disease and accidents plagued them daily. John By himself had a bout of swamp fever. A local resident gave a grim description of the ailment: "After eight to ten days of bilious fever, dreadful vomiting, pains in the back and loins, general debility, loss of appetite, jaundice and fits of trembling would set in. At this time the patient is so cold that nothing will warm him. Our very bones ache, teeth chatter, the ribs are sore, continuing thus in great agony for about an hour and a half; we then commonly have vomit, the trembling ends and a profuse sweat ensues, which lasts for two hours or longer." Workers who did not survive the experience were buried in unmarked graves along the canal route.

It was into this colonial wilderness that John By had brought his family, and the town grew around them. At first, the town was just jokingly referred to as Bytown, but the name stuck. For the following six years, By lived with his wife Esther and their daughters Esther and Harriet on the eastern heights overlooking the entrance locks to the Rideau Canal. During the time the Bys lived there, the location was known as Colonel's Hill. It became Major's Hill when Major Daniel Bolton succeeded John By and moved into the house in 1832. The house burned down in the mid-1850s. Today, the area is called Major's Hill Park, and is one of the best places to view the eight-step locks.

Further to the west was Barracks Hill, later called Parliament Hill. There, wooden barracks for the royal sappers and miners were constructed at a cost of £499. In addition, there was a hospital, a guardhouse, and a parade ground. The structures and grounds were surrounded by a 12-foot-high stockade of sharpened cedar posts. No military battles were ever fought there, however. Instead, the site was the venue for public festivities, parades, open-air concerts, and bonfires. Today, the battles are verbal and the grounds are used for Canada Day celebrations.

In 1826, John By hired Henry Burgess, a young Englishman who came highly recommended, as his clerk. Burgess was granted a raise shortly after, and in 1829 he was

Lieutenant-Colonel John By, circa 1828, founder of Bytown.

given a letter of commendation. After that, Burgess' conduct deteriorated with bouts of drinking, fighting, insubordination, absenteeism, and faulty work. Next, he was thrown out of his lodgings. Burgess handed in his resignation but By refused to accept it. His second resignation met with more success. The lieutenant-colonel dismissed him for neglect of duty. Burgess denied all accusations. He then demanded payment through to the end of his contract. When he didn't receive satisfaction, Burgess threatened to tell the governor-in-chief that By had misappropriated funds. In 1831, he appealed directly to the Board of Ordinance in London, England, saying that he was being punished because he refused to condone By's fraudulent actions.

"I am," Burgess wrote, "the only person alive who can truly explain the accounts for the construction of the works." In addition, he wanted the Board to pay for him to go to London to relate "the most clear and satisfactory statements as to the correctness of Lieutenant-Colonel By's purchasing in many instances and [can] point out on the original vouchers many transactions which cannot be denied." He got his trip to London.

The ongoing expenses for the Rideau Canal were not popular with the British Government, or with the public. Consequently, tales about By paying his private bills with public funds, making false entries, and escalating costs intrigued many people. The Board of Ordinance ordered a closed inquiry into the matter. They found no evidence of

wrongdoing. In 1832, the Board fully exonerated the lieutenant-colonel and pointed out that Burgess was "labouring
under a mental delusion."

But that was not the end of John By's troubles. He was
working in a distant colony to build a major waterway, with
few resources. By had little time to spare, but was hampered
by a ponderous bureaucracy back home in England, as well
as slow communications across the Atlantic Ocean. Small
wonder the politicians and military brass back in London
thought things were going wrong. In addition to handling
day-to-day construction and excavation problems, By was in
an administrative battle, trying to get wider steamboat-sized
locks approved by his superiors. In a forward-looking initiative, the lieutenant-colonel wanted a system of larger locks
that could handle bigger boats, even though the original idea
for the Rideau Canal was that it function as a small boat
route. Finally, the Board of Ordinance grudgingly accepted
locks that were deep enough to accommodate the new naval
steamboats, which were the future of water transport.

In total, the canal needed 47 locks and 52 dams to
control the water level along its entire route. Costs for this
colonial project were adding up fast. The usual accounting
procedure was to have equal annual parliamentary grants to
pay for construction work. John By took a new approach. He
decided not to wait for annual approvals, but to hire contractors as needed. By the end of the project, the total costs
would equal the total annual payments.

Another innovative procedure By used in canal construction was the hiring of civilian contractors in addition to his military personnel. Contractors for excavations were often inexperienced, and some contracts had to be terminated with bothersome legal procedures. On the other hand, five private contractors chosen to do masonry work — Robert Drummond, Thomas MacKay, Thomas Phillips, John Redpath, and Andrew White — were so good that By presented them with silver cups on completion of their work.

Expenditures continued to increase. Due to the difficulty of the work, cost overruns plagued By. Based on the original cost estimate of £169,000, Parliament had approved an initial expenditure of £41,000 for 1827. The same amount was approved for each of the next three years. But Lieutenant-Colonel By soon wanted £528,000. The Board of Ordinance ordered him to stop work. However, it took months for this order to get to him in the middle of the wilderness. In the meantime, a commission appointed by the Treasury Board in 1828 found By's estimates were correct. Then another problem arose. Money to cover By's military staff and barracks would not come from a separate fund but would be taken from the already overspent original canal budget. This added another £60,000 to canal costs.

The final bill for the Rideau Canal would be a staggering one million pounds, the largest amount the British Government had spent on any project in the Canadian colonies. This was so far over the original low estimate that

41

the British House of Commons, in true government fashion, appointed a committee to investigate. The committee had to admit that the work had been conducted with care and economy. However, their report expressed regret that the final cost had been so far over the original estimate. By did not consider the cost extravagant. Nor did he believe that he had wilfully disobeyed orders.

Slow communications were an ongoing problem for John By. The time it took to get government approval from London for different stages of the canal's construction dragged on and on. At the time, all communications went by sailing ship, and the waiting was painful. Determined to get the work done, By did not wait. When he'd been given the assignment, Wellington had instructed him "not to wait for Parliamentary grants but to proceed with all dispatch consistent with economy." So By pushed ahead with the work and prepared to construct the larger locks.

Life in Upper Canada around that time could be both frightening and humorous. In the winter of 1827, By and one of his contractors set out on a week-long trek to check developments along the canal route. The weather was bitterly cold, and sleeping outside was an unpleasant experience, even for two men accustomed to roughing it in the bush. Early one evening, they were elated to come across an American settler's house, where they were invited in to spend the night. Their joy was short-lived. According to John MacTaggart, By's travelling companion on that occasion, they found the house full of people: "Such an ugly, suspicious, dirty-looking set I had never seen before." Not only were they surrounded by unsavoury characters, but there was no place to sit down, much less to lie down and try to sleep. They were told they would find a spot upstairs where they could lie on the floor with their blankets.

Slowly, By and MacTaggart edged their way around the main floor and up a narrow, crooked staircase to a large unheated room with broken windows. There were already some men curled up on the floor. By and MacTaggart immediately noticed a blanket-covered lump on top of a table in the middle of the room. By walked over and lifted a corner of the blanket. To his horror, there lay the body of a teenage boy. He had been shot dead. The lieutenant-colonel placed the blanket back over the body and stomped down the stairs with MacTaggart in tow. He intended to question the owner of the house. But the man was gone. In fact, all the guests had gone. It was not because they feared the military law By represented. It was because they too found the place unacceptable and wanted a warmer (not to mention safer) place to spend the night.

The next morning, after a restless night, By was beseeched by the boy's parents to do something about their son's murder. Sadly, he could do nothing. There was little chance of finding those responsible and even less chance of bringing them to justice in this wild part of the colony. No men could be spared to search the woods for suspects, and no legal system reached very far beyond the settlements of

Kingston or Perth. By and MacTaggart were forced to continue on their way, leaving the parents to bury their boy.

Alexander McNab, another independent contractor on the canal project, recounted one instance when John By demonstrated great decisiveness in keeping a steady grip on the social affairs of his workmen in Bytown. As the story went, some "loose women" had set up business in a rough wooden shanty near the banks of the canal. They were, in By's view, plying their trade so well that they were separating his sappers and miners not only from their money, but from their morals as well. Since these men were key to the surveying, trench digging, building, and rock blasting, he wanted them to concentrate on their work rather than on recreational activities. In addition, By felt that if he could live up to high moral standards, his men should do likewise.

So, early one Sunday morning (the only day of the week when the men could sleep in) the lieutenant-colonel ordered a detachment of his soldiers to march over and demolish the shanty. This they did — probably with more regret than enthusiasm. The proprietress was not amused. Pandemonium reigned as the women scrambled to gather their few belongings and run for safety. A crowd assembled to watch the drama unfold. Some cheered for the soldiers. Others cheered for the shady shanty-ladies. The madam-in-charge proceeded to the Magistrate's Office to sue Lieutenant-Colonel By for damages to her property and disruption to her business. Unfortunately, history has not recorded the outcome of this legal action. All that was recorded, correctly or not, was that John By once again found himself charged with inappropriate conduct.

Canal work continued to progress quickly. The entrance locks and the Rideau River stretch of the waterway were complete by 1831. A steamboat could now cover, in a few hours, the distance it had previously taken days to tramp over by foot. John By was pleased and held a celebration banquet. The main course was ox, "properly prepared and roasted whole." But the final triumph was yet to come. By had expected that the entire project would be done by 1831. However, he had to postpone the grand event because a local miller (using initiative the lieutenant-colonel would have appreciated under different circumstances) had constructed a temporary dam across the river to raise the water level so repair work on his mills could be completed. With winter fast approaching, it was clear that the grand opening of the Rideau Canal would have to wait until the spring of 1832.

Finally, at four o'clock on the afternoon of May 24, 1832, the steamship *Pumper* (renamed *Rideau* for the occasion), preceded by the naval cutter *Rattlesnake*, approached the Kingston end of the Rideau Canal. The 80-foot steamship made its ceremonial passage to Bytown to officially open the recently completed waterway. Onboard were Lieutenant-Colonel John By, his wife Esther and their two daughters, Captain Briscoe of the Royal Engineers, Robert Drummond, builder of the *Pumper* and contractor for the Kingston

Mills Lock, as well as other local dignitaries.

A large noisy crowd had come out to send them off on their journey. It would mark the end of the costly six-year project linking Montreal, and the St. Lawrence and Ottawa Rivers via the Rideau and Cataraqui River system, with Kingston. At each lock station along the way, settlers came out to see the lieutenant-colonel steam past. They waved and he waved back. At Chaffey's Locks, a small party of Natives gathered in their canoes to see the man who had changed their portage route into a waterway. Powered by a 12-horse-power engine, and sporting improvised accommodations for passengers, the *Rideau* triumphantly reached the top of the flight of eight entrancelocks at Bytown five days later, on May 29. Lieutenant-Colonel By had completed his mission.

Upon hearing that By was going back to England, Philemon Wright sought to settle outstanding financial accounts with him. Wright had been one of the private con-tractors hired to work on the canal. Wright's contract had included the difficult Hog's Back Dam, which he was unable to successfully complete. Lieutenant-Colonel By had removed Wright's firm from the dam and had the work com-pleted by a crew of royal sappers and miners. Building the Hog's Back Dam was no easy task. His men worked all winter. But they did not realize that the clay they used contained ice. The ice thawed in the spring, causing the dam to leak. By rushed in to inspect the damage and narrowly escaped being swept away when the dam burst. The structure was rebuilt and, like all of By's work, it is still standing today. Wright and By had a long and bitter argument about extra payments, which Wright felt he was owed. The lieutenant-colonel disagreed, and Wright was left with a low opinion of By's honour.

Lieutenant-Colonel By received firm orders to return to England in August 1832. Around that time, he began to hear more rumours that his canal project was under fire — not by attacking Americans, but by his own government back home. In an effort to deflect some of the criticism, and knowing he had done a good job, By invited the lieutenant governor from Quebec City to accompany him on an inspection tour of the canal. The lieutenant governor declined.

Nevertheless, there were many tributes to By's work. The citizens of Montreal and Kingston were thrilled with the construction of the Rideau Canal. The Montreal Committee of Trade effusively called the canal, "An undertaking of great magnitude and importance, the successful accomplishment of which, in so comparatively short a period, notwithstanding the unheard of inestimable difficulties and impediments which had to be encountered and surmounted, in an almost unexplored and uninhabited wilderness."

Unfortunately, the enthusiastic treatment accorded John By in the colony was not carried over on his return to England. Expecting praise, he was charged instead with overspending and with disobeying orders. However, with the time lag in communications, By did not know about all the trouble coming his way. He thought he had done a good job. And he had. The problem was that the bureaucracy above him did not think so. John By arrived back in England only to face disgrace. By the time the government got the facts right, the damage had been done. And, unfortunately, senior officers and friends who supported By in private failed to do so in public.

John By had left Upper Canada a competent engineer. He arrived in England a political scapegoat. His career was ruined by charges of misconduct and overspending. Even his mentor, the Duke of Wellington, was unable to protect him.

By lived quietly on his farm near the village of Frant and went about increasing his land holdings. The former lieutenant-governor became a church warden and spent his time visiting with friends and family in London.

Four years after completing the Rideau Canal Project, By passed away from the effects of a severe stroke. He died without regaining consciousness. In 1855, Bytown was renamed Ottawa. And for over a century, the master builder of the Rideau Canal was all but forgotten.

Although never used for its intended purpose (a military supply route), By's Rideau Canal did serve as a modest commercial waterway for passengers and freight before the development of roads and railways. It brought settlers into central Canada and carried their produce out. Without the canal, lumbermen, farmers, and shopkeepers, as well as the entire natural resources economy of central Canada, would not have survived and thrived.

Taking only six years to complete, the Rideau Canal has endured, and is now a route for pleasure boats in summer and ice skaters in winter. It is the oldest continuously operated canal system in North America, and its stonework and manual crab-winch lock system are admired by waterway travellers to this day. The canal links the colonial capital of Kingston with the current capital of Ottawa.

In 1926, the Rideau Canal was designated a National Historic Site. In the year 2000, it was declared a Canadian Heritage River. Without a doubt, Lieutenant-Colonel John By had been the right man for the job.

Not only did the lieutenant-colonel create a national treasure in the Rideau Canal, he established a settlement that would become the terminus for the timber industry of the Ottawa Valley, as well as the Capital of Canada.

Chapter 3
Thomas MacKay
(1792 – 1855)

"Such were the men, and such alone,
Who quarried the vast piles of stone,
Those mighty, ponderous, cut-stone blocks,
With which MacKay built up the Locks."
William Pittman Lett,
poet and first City Clerk of Ottawa, 1894

homas MacKay was born in Perth, Scotland. During his early years, he apprenticed to learn the trade of stonemasonry. In 1813 he married Ann Crichton, and four years later the couple immigrated to Canada, settling in Montreal. There, MacKay perfected his craft and entered into a partnership with another Scot, John Redpath. After successfully working together, the two master masons won the contract to build the Lachine Canal in Montreal. Despite this achievement, MacKay was still considered a mere

labourer by the elite of pioneer society.

In 1826, Lieutenant-Colonel John By arrived in the area with orders to build the Rideau Canal. MacKay bid on some of the stonework, and was given the contract to construct the first eight connecting head locks of the canal. The locks led up, like a flight of enormous stairs, from the entrance bay on the Ottawa River. MacKay also won the contract to build the Commissariat Building (to be built beside the canal entrance locks), which was intended to house supplies and workshops for the carpenters, masons, and smiths. In addition, he had the contract for the administration offices, which were also located beside the locks. He also built the two stone arches of the Union Bridge that joined the Upper Town and Lower Town sections of Bytown.

Aside from being a conscientious worker, MacKay was born a lucky man. People said he had "the magic." Everything he touched seemed to be a success. After signing the contract to build the canal entrance locks, he discovered that all the stone he needed to complete the job was already on-site. As the ground was dug out for the canal trench, the stone material became exposed. It was right on hand. However, Lieutenant-Colonel By felt that the stones in the area of Wright's Town were best suited for the work. The lieutenant-colonel had to be persuaded that the canal-site stones were comparable, if not superior. Only after extensive testing did MacKay convince By to change his plans. As a result, there was no need for the time-consuming and expensive task of hauling in large blocks of stone from distant locations. Building the canal locks was as simple as rearranging the rocks. The reduction in cost meant greater profits for MacKay. And this windfall laid the foundation for his financial and social success.

Next came a second stroke of incredible luck. Right across the Ottawa River was a quarry with stone and gravel for making mortar. Not only was it close to MacKay's construction site, but the mortar it made was superior to the more expensive kind he had been importing from England. This unexpected circumstance allowed MacKay — a perfectionist who did not believe in cutting corners to make a profit — to do a good job with less expense and effort.

The Commissariat Building MacKay constructed in 1827 took only six months to finish. This building is Ottawa's oldest existing stone structure and is presently the home of the Bytown Museum. Its stone, mortar, and timber were all found locally. Its joints are held by dowels, as no nails were used anywhere in the structure. In 1854, 22 years after the canal opened, both the Rideau Canal and the Commissariat Building were given to the Canadian Government by the British Government. The building's plaque reads, in part: "Its superb masonry and solid construction are typical of the stonework done by Scottish masons along the Rideau Canal, and, at a later date, on private homes in eastern Ontario."

The bridge arches over the canal, built by MacKay's crew and By's military sappers, were demolished in 1912.

Thomas MacKay

This demolition allowed for the development of Confederation Square and an adjacent parkland to beautify the heart of Ottawa. The act of tearing this structure down, however, was a most difficult task. As the *Ottawa Free Press* reported: "So hard was the stone and so clinging and steel-like the grip of the ancient cement that even dynamite failed to wreck it. As a last resort, the contractors used a derrick to hoist up a block of stone weighing about two tons to a height of fifty feet and [dropped] it on the bridge. For three and a half hours it withstood this terrific battering ... Finally, one last blow carried the entire bridge into the canal; the noise resounding over the city like the boom of a great gun."

A strong admirer of the quality of MacKay's work, and the speed with which it was accomplished, By gave him the contract for the two Hartwell Locks near Hog's Back Falls along the canal to the west.

Using surplus stones from the excavation of the locks, MacKay also built the settlement's first stone church, St. Andrews, at Kent and Wellington Streets. He enlisted the volunteer help of Scottish stonemasons who were idle at the time. They were awaiting orders from the British Government to widen the locks. The masons completed the 13-metre by 16-metre structure in one week.

When the canal work was complete, MacKay got another job from Lieutenant-Colonel By. He began construction on John By's residence, a two-storey building with a commanding view of the Ottawa River.

Life in Bytown was rough, especially in winter. For those with money and some aspirations towards respectability, such as Thomas MacKay and his Scottish stonemasons, accommodations could be arranged in private houses. However, the common labourers stayed in the civilian barracks in Lower Town and often spent the winter in misery and poverty. The priorities in Bytown were primarily the military and engineering projects, followed by land issues, and lastly by the needs of its residents. One Scottish mason, writing back to Glasgow, complained, "Respectable tradesmen [had] been dragged by fallacious hopes and futile expectations to a spot where they had to be crammed into a habitation of three small apartments serving a set of drunken and dissipated beings to the number of nearly 200 or adopt the dreadful alternative of lying under the canopy of an unsheltered Canadian sky at the risk of being frozen to death."

By the early 1830s, MacKay had invested his profits from the original canal work and had begun to build his own settlement for workers on the eastern side of the Rideau Falls (where the Rideau River pours into the Ottawa River). Taking advantage of water power, he erected several mills and founded a village, which he named New Edinburgh.

MacKay's settlement was another addition to the growing community around Bytown. Like Wright's Town to the north, New Edinburgh was a family town based on farming and hydraulic industrial mills. MacKay urged other Scots in the area to join him, and soon the little village developed into

Thomas MacKay, member of the Legislative Council
and founder of New Edinbugh.

a flourishing centre with an industrial complex that included two sawmills, a distillery, a grist mill, and a cloth factory. It also had facilities for manufacturing laths, shingles, staves, sashes, and doors. By this time, its founder was financially secure.

MacKay began to focus on developing his other talents, such as playing the bagpipes. He also enjoyed entertaining around the dinner table and talking over drinks by the fireplace. He often described the working conditions in the bush:

The weather was cold and when night came on we sent two of the axemen ahead to rig a shanty by the side of a swamp. We generally camped near a swamp where water could be had and where the hemlock boughs grew more bushy as we used these to cover the shanty. We also found dry cedar there which makes excellent firewood. When we arrived at the camp we found a comfortable shelter with a blazing fire in front of it. We lay down on the hemlock, holding pork before the fire on wooden prongs while plenty of tea was thrown into a kettle of boiling water. The tin mug, our only tea cup, went round and round till all had drunk and then we went to sleep … Reclining thus, like a parcel of spoons, our feet to the fire, we found the hair of our head often frozen to the place where we lay. For several days together did we lie in these wild places.

Thomas MacKay

MacKay had several wilderness adventures in his new homeland. Among them was a canoe trip over the entire 200-kilometre route of the Rideau Canal system to Kingston. The trip, made with a military survey company under the personal command of Lieutenant-Colonel By, was undertaken after the excavation for the first eight head locks was complete (but before work had started on any other part of the canal). It involved running rapids in birchbark canoes and hacking out portages.

After one of their adventures, MacKay, By, and the crew had to hurry back to Bytown to greet Sir John Franklin, who was travelling down the Ottawa River after one of his attempts to locate a northwest passage. That summer, MacKay also built his first house for his wife Ann and their children, who were coming up from Montreal. This double-frame building wasn't up to the standard of his later stone "castle," but it was better than a tent on Nepean Point (Colonel By was still living in one with his wife and two daughters). The locals began calling MacKay the Laird of New Edinburgh.

In his never-ending search for perfection, he opened the region's first cloth factory in 1841. The blankets woven at MacKay's New Edinburgh factory were of extremely high quality. They won a gold medal in an international competition at the Exposition of All Nations held in London, England, in 1850. For the first six years, all weaving was done on hand looms. Power looms were later installed to take advantage of the ready water power and to boost production. His blankets had found a worldwide market.

Many of MacKay's fine stone buildings were leased to other entrepreneurs as commercial establishments. As these filled up, he built more. MacKay often pointed out to new arrivals that the first rough dwelling a settler put up was called a "shanty." The next, which was more genteel, was called a "log house," and the third, and last, was called a "clapboard house." Personally, he preferred stone.

MacKay was a promoter of the Prescott and Bytown Railway, which connected Bytown to the St. Lawrence and United States markets. Like other local entrepreneurs, he wanted to deliver lumber to the Americans and bring back manufactured goods. He also knew that rail service to New Edinburgh would be a great benefit to the village's economy. The railway would compete with the Ottawa River as a transportation route and, given the high cost of water transport and the winter freeze-up, MacKay thought he had a winner. But progress on the Bytown and Prescott was slow, and the sawmills at the Chaudière Falls were outperforming those near New Edinburgh. In addition, freight rates for lumber barges on the river had dropped from six dollars to three dollars per 1000 board feet. The railway was no longer competitive. The Bytown and Prescott Railway held on for seven years until it was bankrupt. It was then bought by the Grand Trunk Railway.

Although the railway failed, the American market for sawn lumber was booming. MacKay, with his new sawmill with 40 saws producing 40,000 board feet a day, hit upon the idea of using American vessels to transport his lumber south. That first year he lost money, but in the second year his New Edinburgh mills shipped 2.4 million feet of lumber. Once it became clear that the American market was profitable, other area lumbermen joined in, notably the Wrights. American companies also partnered with local businessmen. They began to rent and operate mills such as MacKay's at Rideau Falls near New Edinburgh.

In 1837, MacKay purchased 1100 acres of bush land. It was originally known as MacKay's Bush and later as Rockcliffe Park. Rockcliffe was to become Ottawa's most exclusive residential neighbourhood. Near the western edge of the property he built his own residence, an 11-room stone mansion on the bank of the Rideau River, and named it Rideau Hall. Locals called it "MacKay's Castle," and it quickly became the social centre of the area. MacKay and his family lived there until 1855. Then, about 10 years later, the Government of Canada leased Rideau Hall from MacKay's estate to be used as the official residence of Governor General Lord Monck. Later, the government bought the mansion outright for $82,000 and started a series of expansions to accommodate all the official functions that would be held there. Today, Rideau Hall remains the official residence of Canada's governor general.

Another stone mansion, built by Thomas MacKay for his daughter Annie and her n'er-do-well husband John

MacKinnon, was called Earnscliffe. This mansion eventually became the residence of Canada's first prime minister, Sir John A. MacDonald. Prior to this, the three-storey house was heavily mortgaged when MacKay's son-in-law died without a will. Thomas Keefer, another MacKay son-in-law (who was a much better money manager than MacKinnon), came to Annie's rescue by purchasing the house at auction in 1866 for $48 cash. He assumed the existing $6000 mortgage. Keefer let Annie live there with her family until they could move in with her mother, who was then at Rockcliffe Manor.

Keefer then sold Earnscliffe to an Englishman who had made money on the railroad. Although the new owner put a lot of money into improvements, ill health forced him to return to England. Next, Sir John A. MacDonald rented the house. He liked it so much he bought it. But the Earnscliffe saga has one more twist. In 1873, after his wife died, Thomas Keefer married Annie. They moved into Rockcliffe Manor, where they lived for 30 years.

Thomas MacKay had an active public life and was a major contributor to the improvement and expansion of Bytown. In 1838, he renovated a stone building that once housed workers, and turned it into the town's first school-house. MacKay built the first courthouse and gaol (jail) on Nicholas Street. He also served on Bytown's first municipal council, represented Russell County in the Upper Canada House of Assembly, and was appointed to the Legislative Council of Canada.

Thomas MacKay

Thomas MacKay died in 1855 and is buried in the family vault in Beechwood Cemetery in the east end of Ottawa. Although none of his sons lived to carry on the family business, many streets today in the New Edinburgh neighbourhood of Ottawa are named in honour of his wife and their 16 children. There are streets in the northeast section called Ann, John, Charles, Victoria, Alexander, Thomas, Crichton, and MacKay.

John By and his master stonemason Thomas MacKay had built the infrastructure that would support the growing lumber industry and the expanding settlements in the area. Thus, both of these titans laid the foundation for future entrepreneurs such as Nicholas Sparks.

Chapter 4
Nicholas Sparks
(1792 – 1862)

"That as poor human nature ran,
He was an honest, upright man.
Close fisted as the need occurred,
Yet one who always kept his word."
William Pittman Lett,
poet and first City Clerk of Ottawa, 1894

icholas Sparks, the son of a farmer and horse breeder, was born in Darragh County, Wexford, Ireland. He came from a long line of men called Nicholas Sparks, all the way back to his great, great, great grandfather. With £100 from his family, he set out for Canada, and in 1816 began working as a farmhand for Philemon Wright. Sparks worked for Wright for five years, earning $120 in American funds the first year and £50 in British sterling per year after that. Still, the pay was better than what he would have earned back home. Three years

after arriving in Wright's Town, Sparks had proven himself trustworthy and began travelling to Montreal and Quebec City to purchase supplies for his employer.

In 1821, Sparks married Sarah Olmstead, the widow of Philemon Wright Jr., who had been killed in a stagecoach accident. The newlyweds moved across the Ottawa River, where Sparks bought 200 acres of land for £95 from John Burrows Honey. Honey had just learned that he'd been left an inheritance back in England and was anxious to leave. Wanting to raise money to pay for his passage back home, Honey had initially tried to interest Philemon Wright in purchasing his land. But Wright had seen little value in the area and had turned him down. Sparks, however, wanted to rise above being a paid employee and bought the land even though he had to borrow from Wright to do so. The documents were drawn up and Sparks became the new owner.

He is purported to have wept when he saw his property for the first time. And his friends derided him for his folly. The high plateau he now owned was mainly limestone with one log house and little soil cover. A few trees and cedar bushes grew in rocky crevices. The Town Clerk's office noted that Sparks had been assessed with "eight acres cultivated and 192 acres of wild land." It was not an auspicious start, but Sparks was not one to waste time on self-pity. He quickly set to work clearing a small piece of his new land.

The area surrounding his property was also dismal. A cedar swamp and beaver pond were to the east. To the south were bogs and wood all the way to Dow's Swamp and Hog's Back Falls. To the west there was a store and a tavern at Richmond Landing. To the north were bleak headlands and bluffs falling down to the Ottawa River. However, Sparks' property was situated on a section just south of the headlands, which were called Barracks Hill (now known as Parliament Hill). His holdings would eventually become a prime strip of real estate in what is now downtown Ottawa. The land Sparks bought is now worth billions of dollars.

Almost immediately, Sparks' gamble began to earn him great profits. Intending the land for farming, he was more than a little pleased when he discovered that it would be worth a considerable fortune when Lieutenant-Colonel By arrived to establish a supply town and build the Rideau Canal. Up until then, the settlement had been growing like most pioneer villages, slowly, and without any organized plan. In a few months, By had laid out the pattern of roads and blocks for housing. Sparks soon discovered, much to his great joy, that his 200 acres were entirely within the boundaries of this new town. Furthermore, they had the added advantage of being high and dry. While not good for farming, his land was ideal for building. According to the fortunate Mr. Sparks, "Once you own land, my friends, the wind never blows so cold again."

Nicholas Sparks was an enthusiastic developer from the very start and demonstrated a generous but shrewd approach to his disposition of property. He immediately set

Nicholas Sparks

about surveying his land, designating a main street (which he named after himself), and selling off lots. His intention was to make his part of Bytown its commercial and residential heart. He provided a canal right-of-way and a road allowance for Wellington Street by Barracks Hill. Sparks then set aside land for a market in the east, as well as a location for a city hall, a jail, and a courthouse. Having taken care of his business plan, he gave land on the western side of his property to the Anglican and Presbyterian Churches. Sparks not only benefited from an increase in land prices, he then experienced a change in his social status. He became one of the Ottawa gentry. However, he still enjoyed rowdy conversation over a few glasses of whisky with raftsmen in the local tavern while proposing the most economical ways to transport lumber to Quebec City.

Dividing his land into even smaller urban lots, Sparks willingly donated 20 acres to allow construction of the canal, knowing that during construction and after completion it would be a bonanza for any businesses located in the developing community. Soon, Sparks was selling modest parcels of land to new settlers. By 1836, he was selling lots one-seventh of an acre in size for £400. The loan from Wright to purchase the original land had long ago been repaid in full. Nicholas Sparks rapidly accumulated significant financial resources — and became Bytown's first tycoon.

Recognizing that not everyone was as fortunate as him, Sparks began lending seed money to other newcomers. Aside from the initial sale of the land, he reaped even more profits with the interest on loans that he made to these newcomers. He wrote, "I recall one debtor could not repay me and I repossessed the land I had helped him buy. Before my next meal, I had sold it for 600 pounds though the debt had been only 75 pounds."

Sparks was known to supply free lumber to his friends so they could build their first cabins. And when the Methodist Chapel burned down, he offered the congregation land in another location. Although he was a clever business-man and insisted on being paid promptly, he was not inclined to settle many of his own debts in a speedy manner. In 1834, he was successfully sued by a fed-up creditor for goods this creditor had delivered but for which he had not been paid. Three years later, the hapless creditor was still attempting to collect payment of the outstanding amount of £2803.

Lieutenant-Colonel By, representing the Imperial Government in England, wanted even more land and attempted to buy it from Nicholas Sparks. However, By thought Sparks' price was too high. So the lieutenant-colonel expropriated (without compensation) some of Sparks' land, approximately 80 acres, to build fortifications at the mouth of the canal on the Ottawa River. These fortifications were never erected. Between 1831 and 1848, Sparks' greatest concern was his legal battle with the Board of Ordinance to have his expropriated land returned to him. More land had been taken than was necessary for canal purposes, and Sparks wanted it back. The battle became known as the Rideau Canal Dispute.

The takeover of Sparks' land was, at best, questionable. It included plans for docks larger than those in London, England, as well as a harbour — one that would have required water to run uphill. The Board of Ordinance had taken the best commercial area in Sparks' freehold property, land that was essential to both his commercial aspirations and those of the Upper Town merchants. For almost 20 years, battles were fought over this issue in the courts, in the legislatures, and in the streets.

Sparks proceeded on all fronts. He sued By for trespass and he sued the officers of the Ordinance Department who occupied his land. He organized petitions and lobbied local members of the Legislature to raise the issue in the Assembly. In an irony that was lost on him, Sparks received the same heartless treatment from the military that he dished out to his clients. But the Board of Ordinance was not without blame either. They interpreted the Rideau Canal Act and their agreement with Sparks in an extreme manner. The land ostensibly taken for "canal purposes" was used for barracks, officer quarters, parade grounds, and even a horse pasture.

Sparks believed "right" was on his side. But, according to one ordinance officer, Sparks was a man "of very violent disposition, and weak enough to be led by insidious people." In one instance, Sparks' actions were only stopped by the unexpected arrival of some troops who were en route to Montreal. "He has asserted his intention to take forceful possession of what he calls his property whenever he gets an opportunity, and yesterday while committing the outrage (the occupation of a lock house), sent for raftsmen with directions to give them plenty of Brandy." The Board of Ordinance officer petitioned two magistrates but they refused to act. Ultimately, the officer had to call in the sheriff and the troops.

In 1848, after a Board of Arbitration ruled in Sparks' favour, the expropriated part of his land was returned to him. Nicholas Sparks was awarded £27,000 in settlement. Now much wiser (and richer), he proceeded to cut Sparks Street right across his property. He sold off even more lots. Sparks had maintained his lumber interests even after he became a land developer. He was listed, in the local directory, as a lumber merchant with a grist mill and sawmill at the Chaudière Falls.

The Rideau Canal Dispute was not the only land problem Nicholas Sparks ran into. In 1830, when all land near the canal was becoming more valuable, Sparks took steps to ensure that his title to the land was secure. His ownership became suspect because the original conveyance could not be registered. The land he had purchased from John Burrows Honey had never been properly recorded in the county registry. Technically, the land had not been Honey's to sell. The legal mess carried on for years. Eventually, a deed was executed containing a recital of the facts in the purchase. In it, approximately 200 acres were (re)sold to Nicholas Sparks for the token sum of "five shillings in lawful coinage of Upper Canada." Sparks now had clear title to the land. He soon set about clearing, farming, and building on parts of it while continuing to work in the lumber business.

When he married Sarah, he had described his occupation on their marriage certificate as "timber merchant." Sparks was one of the first to start lumbering on the south side of the Ottawa River. Philemon Wright's men worked on the north side. Naturally, his marriage into the Wright family strengthened his ties to the leaders of the lumber trade in the area. However, Sparks did not rise to become one of the lumber barons. Instead, he remained a prosperous middle-level timberman for many years. He was one of an interested group of citizens who formed the Ottawa Valley Lumber Association in 1836. They promoted the construction of a bridge between Bytown and Wright's Town to replace the ferry. He also continued his family interest in horses and, at the annual fair held in Bytown, Sparks won a prize for the best draft stallion.

Nicholas Sparks was a major contributor to the development of Bytown and the incorporation of the City of Ottawa. He campaigned, with other residents led by Thomas MacKay, to get a separate judicial district for Bytown. Their reason? They considered it too far to travel to the town of Perth for legal matters. Again, Sparks stepped forward with a magnanimous donation — the land for the new courthouse and gaol. The site he selected was "airy, with an excellent spring of water adjoining."

Sparks was also a founding shareowner in Her Majesty's Theatre, a cultural endeavour on Wellington Street, which ran parallel to Sparks Street. When the promoters were unable to meet their financial obligations to him in 1856, the usually generous Sparks retreated from his sponsorship of the arts. He had his lawyers draw up a demand for immediate payment. Of course, he was more generous on other fronts.

In many ways, Sparks had become the patriarch of Bytown. Although he never had any provincial political ambitions, he was active in the local affairs that closely affected his business interests. He became a justice of the peace, was a member of the first municipal council, then an alderman.

From his roots as a humble farm labourer, Sparks became a wealthy landowner and a man of influence. Plaques in Christ Church Cathedral commemorate Sparks and his generosity. By the time of his death, he was known as a man who had endowed his community with land for vital institutions, and as one who had served his community politically (as an alderman). He had not, however, been able in his lifetime to make his Upper Town land the commercial centre of the city.

Nicholas Sparks died in 1862 and was buried in St. James Cemetery on Aylmer Road in Gatineau, Quebec. He left his business to his son. After his death, his wife and their

Ottawa in 1855, showing the Lower Town from Barracks Hill. The Ottawa River is visible on the left and the locks of the Rideau Canal on the right.

three children — Nicholas, Mary, and Esther — were well taken care of. Sparks' estate included 440 lots valued at $80,686 in Ottawa, as well as property in surrounding townships and the large family home on Sparks Street. And, not to be forgotten, some 78 debtors owed him over $19,000. Tenacity, hard work, and a measure of good luck had made Nicholas Sparks a success story in pioneer Bytown and up the Ottawa Valley.

Chapter 5
John Egan
(1811 – 1857)

"When 'Norway Pine' was number one,
John Egan stands almost alone —
The King of the Grand River, then.
The Wellington of lumber men.
A man of boundless energy,
A vast capacity was he,
All difficulties had to fly,
And cower before his dauntless eye!"
William Pittman Lett,
poet and first City Clerk of Ottawa, 1894

J ohn Egan was born in the town of Lissavahaun, Galway County, Ireland. He immigrated to Canada in 1830, settling in Clarendon Township, in what was then Lower Canada. He soon became depot clerk for Thomas Durrell, a leading lumberman on the Upper Ottawa River. In his early twenties,

Egan was given the responsibility of purchasing supplies and handling administrative tasks for his employer. Egan also made numerous trips into the bush, selling supplies to the lumbering shanties up the Ottawa River. A friendly and affable person, he soon developed a network of friends up and down the line and became knowledgeable about the square timber trade.

Initially, timber was cut by small operators, and the round logs were hauled to water and floated to markets further south along the Ottawa and St. Lawrence Rivers. But as the forests receded, the cost of supplying camps in the bush could only be met by large companies that could also operate sawmills and plants to produce shingles, planks, and other wood products. Wood exported to Britain changed from rough timber for military use in building ships to sawn lumber for commercial use in constructing houses and furnishings.

Egan knew that if he could get his hands on some heavily treed land, he could become a rich man rather than a salaried employee. Deciding to take the plunge and go into business for himself, he opened a store in the Village of Aylmer, on the opposite side of the Ottawa River just north of Bytown. He began by selling supplies to lumbermen, then entered the lumber business himself, cutting red pine. The next year he purchased the land of John Wadsworth, a farmer at the Fourth Chute (rapids) on the Bonnechère River in Upper Canada. There, he built a small camp and service centre in what would later become Eganville. At the same time, he was still the supplier to 36 other timber producers.

Egan was also building dams and timber slides on the Bonnechère River and its tributaries to get his own timber to market. A believer in doing everything at once, he formed John Egan and Company at Aylmer in association with a leading timber exporter at Quebec City. Two other men, whose acquaintance he had made while working in the trade, were also involved.

Although instrumental in establishing Eganville, which still bears his name, Egan never lived there. He considered Aylmer his home base. Nevertheless, Eganville grew from one shanty in the bush in 1825 to an officially recognized village in 1891.

When Egan bought the land, he began to build a timber depot, timber slides, a lumber supply store, a grist mill, and sawmills. He then had the area surveyed and divided into lots. Eganville's early settlers continued to develop the flourishing lumber industry as well as a farming sector.

For many years, Egan's primary interest was in the lumbering of red pine. It was a little more scarce, but much more profitable than white pine. In the early 1840s, a general economic depression in North America and Europe brought his operations to a standstill. But he hung on. With the eventual recovery of markets and prices, Egan's business boomed once again. By 1844, he was sending 2.5 million feet of squared timber to Quebec City. Less than one-fifth of this was reported to have come from Crown lands on which he had the right to cut timber. Egan got his timber by buying up the production of small operators and from area settlers.

Transporting products to market was a major expense for all lumbermen. To enlarge his business and make it easier and faster to get his wood to market in the south, Egan began to spend large amounts of his own money to construct more dams and timber slides in both Upper and Lower Canada around Quyon, Petawawa, and Madawaska.

High waters made moving the logs much simpler than dragging them overland with oxen. As well, timber slides beside rapids allowed the logs to pass through without being broken up and damaged by the rocks. Since the late 1830s, Egan had spent £1300 annually on projects to improve the river for transporting his timber to market. And in 1847, he spent even more, some £9456.

While Egan had invested heavily in his own infrastructure, he also co-operated with other lumbermen of the time to supply their camps and get their products down the Ottawa River. He and his friend Ruggles Wright used each other's logging facilities. Later, Egan joined with two other men to build a wagon road from the small settlement of Arnprior, north of Bytown, to the rapids on the Madawaska River.

With so much money tied up in transporting raw timber, Egan decided it was time to diversify his business, as other lumbermen were doing. He and Ruggles Wright put their own steam-powered vessel at Aylmer on the Ottawa River. They launched the *Emerald* in the spring of 1846. Business was good. Soon another boat, the *Oregon*, was launched to serve the area above some rapids on the river. Later that year, John Egan, along with Ruggles Wright and Joseph Aumond (another lumberman), formed the Union Forwarding Company. The company was incorporated to operate these vessels and to transport goods and passengers around the rapids. The Union Forwarding Company used a horse-drawn tramway known as the Union Railroad.

Also in 1846, Egan built a state-of-the-art sawmill with 14 saws to square timber and make planks at Quyon on the Ottawa River. Next he added a grist mill so that local farmers could pay to have their grain ground closer to where they had grown it. Two years later, he paid to have another two sawmills and a grist mill built on the Madawaska River, plus another grist mill at Eganville.

He then bought an existing carding mill for handling wool to be used in making cloth and blankets. Along with growing grain, some farmers raised sheep, and Egan wanted to get into the agriculture business as well as the lumbering business. Such diversification had worked well for Philemon Wright, and John Egan believed it would also work well for him. In 1853, he went back to his roots and built an even larger sawmill at Quyon. The mill was described as "perhaps the most extensive establishment of the kind on the Ottawa with machinery of the latest pattern."

In line with his attitude of "winning together," even if it meant partnering or at least co-operating with competing companies, Egan was one of a number of local lumbermen who got together for mutual benefit and formed the Ottawa Valley Lumber Association. Another co-operative venture was the Upper Ottawa Improvement Company. This initiative involved all the companies that brought logs down the Ottawa River. They began to do the log drives together, thus avoiding the intensely competitive drives that had become the norm when all the separate crews were racing to be first.

Egan's belief in co-operation and partnering was not limited to his business interests. He was an active member of his own small community and the wider community. And he was not blind to the reality that political office was a great way to promote the Ottawa Valley and the interests of lumbermen in particular. So, when a seat became available, he ran in the general election of 1847–1848 as an independent candidate. Egan was "unpledged to any party," but he did have strong reform sympathies. He won. And at the next election, in 1851, Egan was acclaimed to the Legislative Assembly. He was returned by the voters three years later to represent the newly created constituency of Pontiac. He held the seat by acclamation until his death.

John Egan's political success was attributed to his appeal to a wide group of citizens, and to the practical fact that he held extensive timber limits (licences to cut or remove timber on certain sections of land). He owned vast tracts of land at a time when property was a political attribute.

In his speeches in the Assembly, Egan spoke with passion about matters affecting the Ottawa Valley, which he believed was neglected by the government. In 1852, he was a principal member of a movement to have the timber dues on red pine reduced from a penny to a half-penny per cubic foot. The fee was formally reduced by a provincial Order in Council. (Later, Egan and others faced allegations in the Assembly that they had forced the government to do their bidding by threatening to withhold their support for other legislation.) He also tried (without success) to have the government pay for a small canal in his constituency. He argued that it was a public works project, even though it was clearly advantageous to his business and that of Ruggles Wright. Subsequently, work on the canal was suspended in 1857, after almost half a million dollars had already been spent.

In addition to the Union Railroad, Egan was an early supporter (along with Thomas MacKay) of the Bytown and Prescott Railway, which he claimed would open "a profitable market for manufactured timber" in the United States. With the opening of this link to American railroads, goods could be exported year-round through the ice-free port of Boston at cheaper prices than those being charged for exporting through Montreal. Egan was also a founder of the Bytown and Pembroke Railway Company in the Upper Ottawa Valley. In addition, he was the first president of the Bytown and

Aylmer Union Turnpike Company, which had built a road linking the two towns in 1850.

The square timber industry reached one of its peaks during the 1830s. But the lumber business was subject to giddy highs and depressing lows, and Bytown balanced on the knife's edge. Fortunes were made — and lost — according to the rising and falling demand for timber products in the United States and Europe. The wood producers had no control over this. They could build all the dams and timber slides they wanted but if nobody would buy their timber they were bankrupt.

By the early 1850s, John Egan and Company was on a roll. The firm directly employed 2000 labourers up the Ottawa Valley, as well as providing work to hundreds of farmers who supplied the 1600 oxen and horses used in the bush. In 1852, Egan's timber limits covered over 500 square kilometres, more than any of the others along the Ottawa River. In total, his integrated enterprise employed 3500 men in 100 lumber camps with cash transactions that exceeded two million pounds by 1854. And Egan received all the credit. The *Canadian Merchants' Magazine and Commercial Review* called him the "Napoleon of the Ottawa."

Around this time, a group of lumbermen petitioned the commissioner of Crown Lands so they could sell their hydraulic power on the island near the Chaudière Falls. They also petitioned the commissioner to allow them to lease the water power in the channels flowing by. This would allow lumbermen like Egan and the Wrights to charge other businessmen for the use of channelled water power to run their machinery. Small lumber businesses that wanted to ease their logs around rapids and over waterfalls would then pay to use the timber slides owned by Egan and others. All in all, it was a co-operative and lucrative venture. The chief petitioner was John Egan.

For his efforts in this regard, Egan was presented with a splendid carriage by several American gentlemen who were engaged in building a number of large sawmills at Chaudière Falls. Use of the slides for a fee to transport their logs, and water power to run their mills, were worth a lot more to them than a carriage — no matter how splendid.

Egan was enjoying his financial success. He was the employer of thousands of workers in the Upper Ottawa Valley, and his timber licence was unmatched. This timber licence could be acquired with or without title to the land on which the timber stood. Initially, pioneer settlers received a grant of so-called "free land" from the British government in exchange for removing the forest and growing food. The British government saw the value of the cut trees as simply the use a settler could make of the trees as logs for cabins, furniture, tools, and firewood. On vacant Crown lands, however, cutting permits were issued by the government solely for harvesting pine and oak trees to be used by the Royal Navy for ships and masts. But all things change.

As demand for wood expanded from military to

industrial use, the Crown realized it was sitting on a potential fortune. The exploitation of the forests would bring in substantial revenues. So the government began to issue licences to cut timber on specific lands (timber limits). People would bid on these licences at public auctions, pay the fee, and then pay an additional duty on the wood that was actually cut. John Egan was very successful at assembling huge tracts of these timber limits.

Unfortunately, despite his massive operations, one of the many downturns in the cyclical lumber market hit him hard financially. The British Government repealed preferential tariffs on colonial lumber, and the timber industry in the Ottawa Valley went into another decline. Prime timber limits were being depleted and lumbermen had to source their trees further and further away from main transportation routes such as lakes and rivers. This was much more expensive. Conservation and reforestation were not activities practiced by early settlers or lumbermen — the idea was to cut down the tress, not grow more of them.

This decline in the ready availability of wood, red pine in particular, along with decreasing demand for wood exports (due to new manufacturing techniques and new suppliers), was bad for Egan's business. Both exports and prices had fallen by 30 percent. In 1855, the *Perth Courier* reported that it was widely rumoured that Egan's business had failed. The cause was attributed to his heavy financial involvement with a firm in England that had gone bankrupt, taking Egan's money down with it. To make matters worse, his health was also failing.

After a few years, the square timber trade with Great Britain was replaced by trade with the United States, thanks to a growing demand for sawn pine and spruce plank lumber in the U.S. But it was too late for Egan. He had no ready cash and no line of credit to get back in business. In fact, after his death in 1857, the personal property in his estate was valued at a mere £5000. Ten years later, J.R. Booth bid $45,000 at a public auction and picked up Egan's timber limits on the Madawaska River. These limits later turned out to be worth millions.

When he died at the young age of 46, John Egan was buried in Aylmer, near Bytown. It was a fitting resting place for the man who was an active participant in the civic life of that community. While operating his lumber business, Egan had also served as the first mayor of the municipality. A family man with a wife (the former Anne Margaret Gibson of Bytown), three sons, and five daughters, Egan — a devout Anglican — had believed that every settlement needed a local church to encourage family values. Consequently, he had helped found Christ Church in Aylmer in 1843. On the military side (always a consideration in the colonies), he had been appointed a major in the local militia commanded by Ruggles Wright. John Egan had also served as a committee member of the Bytown Emigration Society, of which Thomas MacKay was president. The society, composed of prominent men who had come to the Canadas and made good, sought to encourage others from "back home" to do likewise.

John Egan was not only a lumberman, he was a conscientious citizen who got involved in the interests of his community. And if these interests could be made to coincide with his business interests, so much the better. Like J.R. Booth and E.B. Eddy, John Egan diversified his core business to take advantage of new opportunities. Unlike Booth and Eddy, he was not able to recoup his fortune after serious business setbacks. Had he lived longer, his story may have had a different outcome.

Chapter 6
J.R. Booth
(1827 – 1925)

*"When I want a thing done, I want it done
the way I say it should be done."*
John Rudolphus Booth

J ohn Rudolphus Booth was born in Canada on a remote farm in Shefford County, Quebec. He was the second oldest of five children born to John Booth and Eleanor Rawley Booth, who were immigrant farmers from Ireland. As a child, Booth enjoyed working with tools. He spent many hours making miniature bridges and working water wheels on the creek that ran through his parents' farm. When he was 21 years old, he decided that farming was not for him, and struck out on his own. His first job, which lasted three years, was working as a carpenter building bridges for the Central Vermont Railway.

During those years, Booth met Rosalinda Cook, who he

married in 1852. Travelling along the Ottawa River in 1854, they arrived in Bytown with nine dollars to their names and took up quarters in a stone house on downtown Queen Street. Booth, known to all as J.R., soon found work as a machinist across the river in Wright's Town. Lacking any other form of transportation, he walked the five kilometres to the shop each day then walked home again after work. In the evenings Booth made wooden shingles, which he sold for extra money.

Just as he had decided that farming was not for him, Booth, who had quickly worked his way up to manager of the machine shop, decided that being a mill employee was not to his liking either. He wanted to be his own boss, so he opened his own machine shop. It was demolished by fire eight months later. Disheartened, but far from giving up, he embarked on a new venture: a shingle mill. When his rent on the mill was suddenly doubled, he bought an abandoned sawmill that had access to water power from the Chaudière Falls on the Ottawa River.

It was then that history and opportunity came together for J.R. Booth. In 1857, Queen Victoria chose Ottawa as the capital of the new Province of Canada. Lumber companies actively tried to outbid each other for the lucrative contract to supply the wood for the construction of the new Parliament Buildings. Booth underbid many larger competitors and secured the contract for himself. Next, he used rather innovative technology to fulfil the terms of the deal.

While other lumbermen used oxen to skid logs and haul supplies in the bush, Booth believed horses would be faster and more agile. He was right. And he eventually ended up owning some 4000 horses.

Booth's ingenious business tactics turned a profit of $15,000 on the Parliament Buildings contract and established J.R. Booth Lumber Company as a major player in the lumber trade. When the British North America Act was ratified by the British House of Commons, Ottawa became the permanent capital of the Dominion of Canada. The capital had a population of 18,000. The brand new Parliament Buildings had been built with the wood from J.R. Booth's mills. Although Booth could have relaxed his efforts, he was determined to keep expanding.

His progressive thinking continued to jolt his rivals. He undercut local lumberjack wages and brought in unemployed longshoremen from Montreal and other parts of Quebec to work in the bush and drive his logs on the river. Referred to by locals as Booth's "dock rats," these men skilfully rode the logs down the river, daringly broke up logjams, and completely outperformed the old-time lumberjacks.

Booth was a short, solidly built, unpretentious man who became slightly stooped as he aged. His piercing blue eyes and shock of white hair were familiar sights in his mills right up until his death at age 99. Never concerned with current fashion, he always wore his clothes until they were well and truly worn out, or as his nephew, J.R.B. Coleman, put it,

Cookery on Booth's raft, circa 1880.

until they were "green with age." Apparently, Booth had an old overcoat that he must have bought as a young man. Whenever a button fell off the coat, he would arrive at Coleman's mother's house (Booth's sister) and have her sew it back on. Booth had an entire household staff in his home on Metcalfe Street in downtown Ottawa, but he took his mending elsewhere. He was a frequent visitor at the Coleman house, partly because Mrs. Coleman also knitted the inside liners for his deerskin mitts. He depended on these mitts, as he was frequently outside checking on his lumber business.

In addition to her domestic skills, Mrs. Coleman was also the family historian. A wealthy man, Booth received many letters from strangers claiming kinship and asking for money. He had no idea who these strangers were, and brought all the letters over to the house for Mrs. Coleman to sort through. Did the petitioners get any money? Nobody knows. But probably not directly. Booth was generous in donations to his church and to a hospital in Ottawa. And he attended to the wages of his workers far more than was the practice at the time. But he did believe that people should work for their money, not have it handed to them.

When the Madawaska timber rights of John Egan came up for auction (they had reverted to the Crown following Egan's death), Booth resolved to get possession of the 650 square kilometres of virgin pine timber — at any price. J.R. Booth had a solid business reputation and he knew it. He decided to seek credit from the manager of the Bank of British North America in Ottawa. The bank manager was not impressed. "What collateral do you have for the loan?" he asked. "These," said Booth, firmly planting his hands on the bank manager's desk. He got the loan.

Before negotiating with the bank, Booth had sent his cousin, Robert Booth, up the line to the Madawaska Valley to have a look at the trees. By one o'clock on the day of the auction in Ottawa, cousin Robert had not yet returned. The auction was to begin at two o'clock. Booth was getting nervous, and so was the bank manager who had come along to keep an eye on the bank's investment. To their vast relief, Robert showed up just after one o'clock with the good news: "Buy at any price. The pine stands like grass. For number and for quality they are unexcelled."

All the lumber barons were present at the auction, and just as anxious as Booth to get their hands on the Egan timber rights. The bidding was hot and heavy. It was usual for bids to be signalled with a hand movement, but earlier that day, Booth had informed the auctioneer that he would indicate his bids with a wink. As the bidding got higher and higher, Booth kept winking and winking, and one by one the opposition dropped out. Eventually, the auctioneer signalled that the Egan Estate limits had been sold for $45,000 to the man dressed in the shabby work clothes of a mill labourer. The other lumber barons thought Booth was foolish to pay so much. But the Egan purchase made Booth his fortune. Years later, he turned down an offer of $1.5 million as "not nearly enough" for the same land.

But Booth did not always come out on top in private deals or at government auctions. In the 1870s, he had passed on buying L'Amable du Fond River limits for $250. The owner was getting married, needed the cash, and was willing to sell for what he had originally paid. Booth was short of money at the time and the deal fell through. Thirty years later, with a larger bank account, he readily paid $565,000 for the same limits.

Booth eventually owned more than 18,000 square

kilometres of forest, making him the largest timber rights owner in the British Empire. By 1892, his mills were turning out 140 million board feet of pine lumber, more than any other mill in the world. His Ottawa mill and lumberyard covered 160 acres. He had 500 wagons, and employed 2000 men in his mills and 4000 men in the bush operations. His lumber went to markets in the United States and England. The deck planking on the renowned ocean liners *Mauretania* (one of the most enduring symbols of ocean liner reliability on the North Atlantic) and her unfortunate sister ship *Lusitania* (which was sunk by a German U-boat during World War I) was made of white pine, which was stencilled with the initials *JRB.*

Booth also used other identifiers to allow his raw timber to be readily spotted amid the jumble of logs leaving the bush. One such identifier (or brand) was in the shape of a turtle, a bark mark he used on all his logs and pulpwood. The turtle symbol was 36 centimetres long. Its body was cut out by a sideways blow of an axe on the side of the log, with each of the four legs cut out with two *V* axe chops. Booth's other identifier was a diamond shape, inside of which were the joined initials *JB.* This brand was driven into the sawn ends of cut logs by a metal stamping hammer.

Before logs were taken to sawmills by train, they were floated downriver in log drives. After the drive had passed, the shoreline had to be "swept" to find lost and abandoned logs. These were loosened and sent on downstream. Logjams often developed in narrow rough sections of the river, and men had to walk out on the logs and break up the jam. It was dangerous work and many lumberjacks were seriously injured or killed. Being a far-sighted man, Booth realized that a boat would be very useful for such a job. But it had to be a strong and manoeuvrable boat with a shallow draught to enable it to work in very little water.

In the 1850s, Booth asked John Cockburn, a shipbuilding immigrant from England, to make him such a boat. Cockburn was up to the challenge. The log-drive boat he designed did the job exceptionally well and became an integral part of the Ottawa Valley lumber scene for almost a century. Ranging from 6 to 16 metres in length, the Cockburn *Pointer* drew only a few centimetres of water and could easily be turned by the use of one oar. The watercraft could run rapids, sweep the shoreline or the shallows for logs, break up a logjam, and be pulled up onshore all with equal ease. Rivermen boasted that the boat "would float on a heavy dew."

As markets for lumber steadily increased, Booth expanded and diversified his business. By 1904, he was moving into the production of pulp and paper. His newsprint paper was sold in Canada, the United States, and Great Britain. To transport his lumber products to market in the American northeast, Booth pressed on to finish building the Canada Atlantic Railway (CAR), which he had begun in 1879. The rail line, often referred to as "Booth's Railway," shortened the existing route from Montreal to Chicago by some 1290 kilometres and gave Ottawa a direct link to the Atlantic coast at Boston. Up until then Booth had relied on barges, which he felt were too slow. The railway was completed in 1896, after 17 years of work. But slow and labour-intensive construction methods proved extremely costly, especially during the cold winter freeze.

Another problem was the St. Lawrence River. For five years, trains were taken across the river on a large ferry, the *Canada Atlantic Transfer*, at Valleyfield, Quebec. This was expensive and time-consuming, and Booth wanted a better way. He wanted a bridge. He finally got a charter to build one and financed the entire construction himself — it cost him $1.3 million. By 1890, after only nine months of work, the first train crossed the new bridge.

Booth was also determined to proceed with construction of a west rail line to Georgian Bay in 1893. The work was completed in three years. But costs were high, especially through the newly designated Algonquin Park, where grades were steep and rock cuts and swamps were numerous. Again, Booth's plan succeeded. The railroad was soon carrying 20 million bushels of western grain and 200,000 tons of flour and freight annually.

J.R. Booth asked the City of Ottawa for a $100,000 bonus for his railway and an additional $50,000 for a new Union Station in the heart of the city. But he was already known for using the carrot-and-the-stick approach in his business dealings. Booth tried to convince councillors that his rail line

John Rudolphus Booth, lumber baron, circa 1898.

would "bring back to Ottawa's merchants and traders their role of supplying the valley." He was certain it would create a grain distribution hub. And that it would, with the use of water power for milling, create a "great flouring centre." The burghers of old Bytown were not convinced.

In 1904, Booth sold the Canada Atlantic Railway to Grand Trunk for $14 million. There was public speculation about his motives. It was rumoured that perhaps the sale was made because Booth disliked political interference in his operations. Or perhaps it was because his two partners had recently died, or because he was disheartened by the accidents and deaths of the workers on the line. As usual, Booth never explained his reasons. However, he was 77 years old at the time. It is possible that he just wanted to give himself a slightly easier job as he got older.

J.R. Booth's relationship with his employees was a paternalistic blend of compassion and sternness. Although what he said went — or else — there are numerous examples of his generosity. His absolute belief that he knew best what his employees needs were was offset by his interest in their well being. Despite Booth's authoritarian attitude and great wealth, his employees felt he was one of them. He could well afford the most extravagant carriage, yet for 50 years he was picked up at home and driven to work in a horse and buggy by the same mill hand, Dave Beauchamp (who was about the same age as his employer). In the winter, they used a horse-drawn sleigh. Although he could have relaxed and indulged himself, Booth never changed his hard-working habits. Nor did he adopt the attitude of the rich. It was only in the last few years of his life that he agreed to be driven to work in an automobile.

J.R. Booth was a dedicated lumberman. He had expanded into the railway and shipping industries only because they complemented his lumber company. Booth involved himself in all aspects of his business and did not believe in retirement, either for himself or for his older employees. In a time long before employment insurance plans and company pensions existed, he gave his employees less strenuous jobs as they got older. He demanded a lot from his employees, but twice as much from himself.

Booth continued to take on physically challenging tasks well into his eighties. One day, at the age of 86, he was supervising 25 men who were blasting out a wheel pit far beneath the Ottawa River at the Chaudière Falls. Suddenly the dam began to collapse. Booth, who did not hear the warning noise because he was going deaf, was pushed to safety by one of his workmen just as the raging torrent of water swept the ladder out from under him. Later that same year, while he was supervising the demolition of a storehouse, a large beam fell and he suffered a compound fracture in his left leg, a badly bruised shoulder, and a severe cut on the left side of his face. But he took it all in stride — it was all in a day's work.

Booth was a progressive employer. In 1895, he reduced his employees' working day from 11 to 10 hours without any decrease in pay. In 1910, he continued to pay his 2000 employees for time lost during a strike on the Grand Trunk Railway. It was, he said, a pity if they had to starve because someone else decided to strike. This humanitarian view cost him over $12,000. Then, in 1911, he stunned the union by reducing the working day for paper millhands to eight hours without the employees even asking.

However, Booth had a hearty dislike for what he considered "meddling" by outsiders. When 400 of his employees briefly went on strike in 1918 because he refused to grant them a pay increase, Booth immediately shot off a letter to the business publication *Canada Lumberman and Woodworker.* In response to a critical editorial that had appeared in a local Ottawa newspaper Booth wrote, in part, "I have not written this letter to boast of what I have done but I do not wish people to think that I have got something for nothing, and that I am unfair to my men with whom I have had the best relations for so many years and shall have again, if outsiders would not seek to stir up strife."

Another anecdote reveals more of his social conscience. His nephew, J.R.B. Coleman, who was studying forestry at university, had briefly worked in one of Booth's lumber camps. On a weekend visit to Uncle J.R.'s private railway car, the young man had commented on the quality of food in the lumber camps: "In the camps all we have is salt pork, no biscuits or anything like that. Down here they eat fresh beef, biscuits, pickles and just about anything they want." Booth hadn't said anything in response, but he did take action. A week later, into the camp kitchens came provisions of fresh meat, barrels of pickles, and biscuit fixings.

A Presbyterian all his life, Booth was a regular church-goer and gave generously to several church causes, declining any public acknowledgement of his gifts. One of his most visible contributions was a large stained glass window, donated in memory of his wife Rosalinda after her death in 1886.

Booth remained an influential member of St. Andrew's Church after his wife passed away. When Canada's Methodist,

Congregational, and Presbyterian Churches were negotiating to form the United Church of Canada, he was driven to the church to cast his vote in opposition. Entering the church and looking around, he commented to the congregation, "If the Methodists want to take this [church] over, I'll build you a better one." The congregation rejected church union.

Because of his strong faith, Booth believed in giving of his time and talent to many worthwhile endeavours. He cared for his workers when there were fires and looked after widows and children when workers were killed on the job. Booth maintained a great interest in hospitals, and helped establish St. Luke's Hospital in downtown Ottawa. He was a major contributor to its operation, built an entire wing, and was the chairman of its board of trustees for many years.

J.R. Booth was a lumberman through and through, but he also had an appreciation for another material: concrete. The huge pulp mills, with which he began to diversify his timber business when he was 75, were all built of concrete. As well, all the buildings erected at his mills in the early 1900s were concrete. Not surprisingly, Booth became a director of the Canada Cement Company.

Still, he never forgot that his core business was lumber and that all his other enterprises grew out of that base. Booth's success was a combination of his commitment to quality, his hard work, his shrewd business mind, and his ability to see potential where others saw only overwhelming odds. He readily acted upon his intuition, but he was never rash. He guarded his credit and his name by acting honestly and consistently in his dealings. And he retained personal control over his diverse holdings until 1921, when, at the age of 94, he agreed to the incorporation of J.R. Booth Limited. His solicitor and three siblings were then appointed as directors along with J.R.

Perhaps Booth's greatest failing was his lifelong tendency to seal a business deal with just a handshake. In 1925, a judgement was rendered against J.R. Booth Limited in the matter of Walter K. McLean, who had undertaken to salvage deadhead logs from the Ottawa River north of the city for the Booth company. For this purpose, McLean built a sawmill, and advances of money were made to him by Booth. In consideration of these advances, McLean assigned the mill in question to J.R. Booth Limited, the deed taking the form of a sale. Eventually McLean pressed a suit for recovery of monies due him under the original contract for salvaging deadheads and sawing lumber. The Booth interests denied all liability and counter sued for $40,000, representing the monies advanced to McLean, which they claimed were only in the nature of a mortgage.

It was a long trial. The Booth lawyers attempted to introduce witnesses in support of their contention but the verbal evidence was thrown out of court. The final judgement ordered Booth to pay McLean the sum of $7050.82, with recourse to a further $1650 not covered by his contract. The counterclaim of $40,000 was dismissed and Booth's company was ordered to pay all costs. It was one of the few times the old titan did not come out on top in a business deal.

J.R. Booth was a study in opposites. He was actively involved in all aspects of his businesses, yet he liked to keep information close to his chest. Though Coleman oversaw much of his uncle's lumber operation, Booth didn't tell his nephew about the Canada Atlantic Transit Company fleet of five ships he had on the Upper Great Lakes to connect with the western leg of his railway business. Maybe it was because he didn't like to brag. Or maybe it was that he didn't fully trust anybody — not even those related to him. But perhaps it was simply because Booth was an extremely private man. He even tried to preserve his privacy after his death by ordering that all his personal and business records be destroyed. While many papers went up in flames, some were (fortunately) spared (those that were already in the hands of other people, that is).

Despite numerous setbacks — including the Great Fire of 1900, in which he lost over 50 million feet of lumber, 20 tenant houses, 6 stables, 4 stone houses, a wagon shop, a paint shop, a machine shop, a blacksmith shop, and a double-decker storehouse that contained 33,000 bushels of oats, 700 tons of hay, and a number of wagons — Booth repeatedly set about rebuilding his empire. His home near the Chaudière Falls, like those of other industrialists at the time, was completely burned in the Great Fire. And, like the other wealthy homeowners, he then moved uptown to Metcalfe

Street to build a new house. In keeping with his motto, God Helps Us, Booth trusted heaven would provide as long as J.R. worked hard to help heaven along.

Booth was a native-born Canadian who became a leading businessman in a forest industry that had previously been dominated by the British and the Americans. Not only did he assemble Canada's largest timber holdings, he also became the biggest manufacturer of lumber for both the United States and British export markets. His contribution to Canadian industry was noted in 1904 in the *American Lumberman*. An article referred to H. Frederick Weyerhaeuser and J.R. Booth as "the two great timber kings of North America."

Booth worked well into his nineties, remaining mentally alert and continually astonishing others with his remarkable memory. In 1919, when J.S. Knapman, a Toronto purchasing agent in the lumber industry, visited Booth at his sawmill, the old man recognized him immediately. Addressing the agent by name, Booth remarked, "Yes, it is just 12 years since you used to come around here ... You bought a good many thousand poles from me for the Bell Telephone Company and I have not seen you since you went out of that business." Knapman was amazed at Booth's recall. But this was just normal business relations for the old man.

At one point in his life, some of Booth's friends, hoping to expand his personal interests, convinced him to go fishing. It was a hopeless quest. Booth soon got bored and discarded his fishing pole to retrieve some logs that had drifted onto the shoreline. Once, in another attempt to get his mind off business, his daughters convinced him to take a two-week vacation in Atlantic City. On day one, Booth claimed he had been up at five o'clock, had seen everything, and that he was going home. And he did just that.

While maintaining a high profile in his business, Booth always retreated from the public eye, regardless of the event. He even skipped the wedding of his granddaughter, Lois Frances Booth, to Prince Erik of Denmark in February 1924. It was the Ottawa society wedding of its time, but Booth simply refused to attend.

Given his dislike of attention, Booth never entered into public life, preferring to wield influence behind the scenes. Often the advisor of businessmen and politicians, he was a leader in forming and supporting several large business organizations. In 1901, the city was buzzing with rumours that a knighthood was to be bestowed on J.R. Booth. In spite of support from his contemporaries for the honour, the knighthood was never given. It was suggested that, even with his position as a confidant to influential people, he was denied a knighthood because he often ran afoul of government regulations. He was, for example, summoned to court (during a certain period) on an almost weekly basis for his refusal to abide by the changing laws on the disposal of waste products from his mills — he dumped them into the Ottawa River.

One of Booth's last public appearances took place in

1920, a few days short of his 93rd birthday. The old man attended a Stanley Cup hockey game between the Ottawa Senators and the Seattle Puckchasers of the Pacific Coast League. He was escorted to centre ice by his grandson, J.R. Booth Jr., where he dropped the puck at the opening face-off. He received a resounding ovation from the 7000 fans and was presented with a large floral horseshoe by the hockey club. This was a most appropriate recognition because Booth's life-long private passion was flowers. He never missed an opportunity to see a flower show. Several years after his death, the Central Experimental Farm in Ottawa began to develop a variety of yellow chrysanthemum in honour of Booth. Fitting, too, because some 465 acres of the Central Experimental Farm's land had been donated by Booth to create the farm in the first place.

At the time of his death, Booth's enterprises consisted of multiple businesses. He was Ottawa's biggest taxpayer and its largest private employer. Though few of his personal papers remain today, his business dealings have become the stuff of legend, with tales of the "old man" being passed down over the decades. Only three of Booth's eight children survived him. They were at his bedside when he passed away on December 8, 1925.

After his death, despite the wishes of his family that no flowers be sent for the funeral, so many people paid their respects through floral arrangements that six automobiles full of flowers followed the funeral procession — quite a tribute to a man who disliked being singled out for his standing in the community.

J.R. Booth's funeral, like the man himself, was plain and modest. The were no pallbearers beside the casket, no music, no singing, no uniforms, no ostentation of any kind. It consisted of a simple service in the St. Andrews Presbyterian Church built by Thomas MacKay and his Scottish stonemasons. The chief mourners were family members and the executives of J.R. Booth Limited. Prime Minister William Lyon Mackenzie King attended, along with a representative of the governor general, the provincial premiers, a number of municipal officials, and hundreds of Booth's former employees. A cortege of 150 cars followed the hearse to the cemetery.

The sawmills at the Chaudière Falls — built, owned, and run by Booth for over seven decades — were silent. Upon hearing of Booth's death, former Prime Minister Arthur Meighen said, in part: "A pioneer in lumbering, in railroad construction, and many other activities, he has given to this Dominion services of a nation-building character and had done much towards alleviating the difficulties of human life. His vision, his unerring judgement, his quiet generosity, and his sincerity made him an outstanding gentleman among his fellows."

Prime Minister Mackenzie King called Booth "a father of Canada" for his contribution in building the economic base of Ottawa. The front pages of the local newspapers described him as a "king," an "emperor of the woods," and a "monarch of the Upper Ottawa." Such accolades attest to Booth's eminence in the early days of Canada's capital.

When Booth left the countryside and his vocation of carpentry to take up residence in Ottawa, he had only nine dollars in his pocket. Seventy-eight years later, he died leaving a business empire worth $44 million dollars.

Chapter 7
E.B. Eddy
(1827 – 1906)

"Hull without the E.B. Eddy Company would be like
Shakespeare's play of Hamlet with Hamlet left out."
A.H.D. Ross in *Ottawa Past and Present*

zra Butler Eddy was born near Bristol, Vermont, and came to the Bytown area after trying his hand at a number of jobs further south. He and his first wife Zaida arrived at their new home around 1854 with very little money. They rented the upper floor of Ruggles Wright's old blacksmith shop and set to work making matches — as well as wooden clothespins and bowls — by hand.

E.B. Eddy was a self-made man who flourished at a time when business was a wide-open arena in which economic gladiators had great successes, disasters, bankruptcies, and new beginnings. He began his career in New York City, where he was a store clerk. He followed this job with various business endeavours between 1847 and 1854. His experience included a dairy products business and the manufacture of matches back in Vermont. None of these ventures were profitable, which may be why Eddy moved north.

Using the "buttings" from discarded pine stubs from the Chaudière Mills, Eddy and his wife worked through the nights in their family business, selecting and hand-dipping the wood to make matches. Zaida taught local women and children how to package the matches in their homes, and they were paid a small amount based on the number of packages they could put together. The matches were sold in a store nearby. Eddy established a full-fledged match factory in 1861 and soon began selling his matches door-to-door throughout the region. Before long his business skills had boosted sales in places as far away as Toronto. According to a long-time associate, George Henry Millen, Ezra Eddy was a born salesman. His success allowed him to diversify the products he shipped by boat on the Rideau Canal to include wooden buckets and washboards as well as matches. Using the profits from these early sales, Eddy purchased machinery to automate his manufacturing process.

In an early division of labour, women dipped each match head individually to coat it with the chemical compounds that would create fire when the match was rubbed on a rough surface. Mixing these volatile chemicals was a dangerous business. This was a man's job. The dipping compounds were placed in a pail, which a male employee

would then hold while bouncing up and down on a spring-
board. It was not a sought-after job and employees were hard
to keep. But the business grew.

As a further indication of his success, E.B. Eddy was able
to buy land from the Wrights, who were getting rid of some
properties to streamline their operations and adapt to changing business requirements. Between 1866 and 1872, Eddy
bought several lots in Hull and near the Chaudière Falls. In
his first step towards getting into the lumber business, he
bought a sawmill from the Wrights. By the early 1870s, Eddy
was in a position to purchase some timber limits and build
his own sawmill near the match factory. He was on his way as
a business titan. His expanding operations in the manufacturing of lumber and the production of a full line of wood
products were spectacular.

The 1870s were the crucial years in Eddy's business rise.
His purchase of timber limits at public auction, facilitated by
money provided by friends and associates in Ottawa, allowed
him to take advantage of the bad situation that was affecting
others. For Eddy, the opportunities were good. In 1873, with
the fall in British and American economies and the resulting
international depression, he was able to get cutting licences
on more than 3600 square kilometres of timber limits along
tributaries of the Ottawa River. He also owned at least one
farm that provided supplies for his lumber camps and
shanties. His match factory, on an island owned by the Wright
family at the Chaudière Falls, produced nearly a million

Ezra Butler Eddy, circa 1873.

matches a day, a mighty output for the time. By 1880, he had purchased three more sawmills and was producing between 50 and 75 million board feet of lumber annually. By then, E.B. Eddy was one of the largest producers in the Ottawa Valley. He became a millionaire 20 years after he had arrived in town.

Eddy's career in politics, like John Egan's, may well have helped his career in the lumber business. It did coincide with the period of greatest growth in his holdings. Well known in Hull Township as a major employer, Eddy ran as the Conservative candidate for the Quebec Legislative Assembly in 1871. He won by 777 votes over his Liberal rival. While victory was sweet, it was short. Running as an Independent candidate in 1875, he lost to his Conservative opponent. Angry voters who were against the incorporation of Hull as a municipality, and the French-speaking settlers who now formed the majority of residents in his constituency, did not vote for him. True to his independent character, Eddy was more concerned with the practical aspects of his business and his riding. In his own words, he "cared very little for political theory." For four years he had been both mayor of Hull Township and a member of the Legislative Assembly, and he had frequently failed to show up to council or assembly meetings because of the demands of his business.

However, he did introduce the bill creating the City of Hull in 1875. When other Ottawa Valley entrepreneurs needed certain access to their timber limits, he lobbied for the

_____

Ottawa Titans

incorporation of the Ottawa and Gatineau Valley Railway Company. During this period, he also served as a director of the Central Canada Railway. The Eddy family, which included two sons and a daughter, was not the social equivalent of the Wrights, but it was definitely part of the new business elite.

Eddy was the largest match manufacturer in the British Empire until a fire destroyed his mills and lumberyard. Almost bankrupt but far from giving up, he proceeded to rebuild two sawmills, a door and window factory, a pulp mill, a match factory, and a foundry, as well as offices and warehouses, with a loan from the Bank of Montreal. In order to get the loan, he had to allow the bank's manager to supervise his financial affairs. Eddy decided to divest himself of some of his remote timber limits, keeping only enough to supply his factories. In 1886, he consolidated his enterprises and incorporated E.B. Eddy Manufacturing Company as a joint-stock company with a capital of $300,000. Eddy was the president and he had four Ottawa partners.

He then began to concentrate on wood pulp by buying the production rights for indurated fibreware (cardboard), which his firm began producing in 1887. Eddy converted the huge grinders, which mechanically chopped up the logs for wood pulp, to a chemical process that produced the pulp. The new Mitscherlich process extracted cellulose from wood by boiling the wood with chemicals. Eddy built his own bisulphate pulp factory and used this new technology to speed up and streamline operations. The factory, equipped with four

110

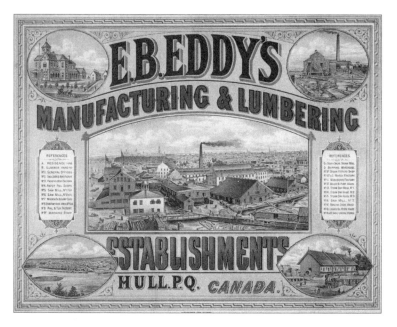

A company advertisement for E. B. Eddy's Manufacturing
& Lumbering Establishments, circa 1884.

"digesters," started operations in 1889. The 50 tons of pulp
his mills spewed out each week was of excellent quality, and
was sold to customers in the United States. He then branched
out into the production of fine papers, installing his first
paper-making machine in 1890. Later, two more machines
were added. And, along with some partners, Eddy built a
paper factory equipped with five machines for making tissue
paper, printing paper, brown paper, and newsprint. In this
way, E. B. Eddy, the "match king," rebounded from the

downturn in the lumber trade, moved into the growth business of pulp, and then expanded into diversified paper manufacturing.

His growing industries needed more land and more power to operate, so Eddy bought additional lots along the Ottawa River and the Chaudière Falls from the Wrights, the City of Hull, and the Quebec Government. By the late 1890s he had consolidated his businesses where he could be assured of hydro-electric power. Thus, Eddy became a major player in the Canadian paper industry.

A ranking member of the business aristocracy, Eddy was influential as an alderman in Hull, the municipality he had helped to create. He served 10 years as alderman. His previous political experience at the provincial level made him a natural choice for various public committees. Eddy was skilled at blending political and financial interests. He offered to pay the interest on city debentures or transfer promissory notes to the municipality. In this way, a number of improvements to the Hull water and electrical system were a direct result of blending the needs of both the Hull citizens and the Eddy companies.

By the end of the 19th century, Eddy was free of debt and all his enterprises were making money. But, due to high insurance costs, he decided to cancel his premiums and self-insure his plants — big mistake.

The Great Fire of 1900 killed seven people in Ottawa and Hull, left 15,000 homeless, destroyed more than 3000 buildings, and caused property damage in excess of $10 million. Before the fire, some of the town's most prosperous people lived in the area around the Chaudière Falls. E.B. Eddy suffered the greatest loss on the Hull side of the river while J.R. Booth lost his mill complex and his fine home on the Ottawa side. The firefighters and the militia were overwhelmed. They tried to use dynamite to make a firebreak amid the closely packed mills and houses. Their plan backfired and the glowing embers were scattered over a wide area, setting off even more fires.

Along with Booth, Eddy was one of the few businessmen to recover from the Great Fire of 1900. His losses were estimated at three million dollars, of which only $150,000 was covered by a few remaining policies and investments. Immediately after the fire, Eddy began to arrange loans that would enable him to rebuild. His own money was not adequate to cover his losses, but he had faced fire before and had come back. He would do so again. The new mills were built with borrowed money.

In 1894, at the age of 67, Eddy, now a widower, married Jennie Grahl Hunter Shirreff of Halifax. It was a union that was later to have repercussions when it came to resolving his estate. A rich man who had been raised a Baptist, Eddy was active in many philanthropic causes in the area, supporting Protestant institutions of all denominations as well as Catholic ones. The main beneficiaries, however, were on the Ottawa side of the river and included the Ottawa Ladies'

College, the Orphans' Home of the City of Ottawa, the County of Carleton General Protestant Hospital, and the Annie Lewis Memorial Convalescent Home for Sick Children of Ottawa.

Always an active man, Eddy continued going to work well into his 70s. He was a Freemason of such stature that a lodge bearing his name had been founded in the 1870s. His astute business sense, his steadfast determination, and his demanding work ethic were acknowledged by his employees and his business colleagues. At a time when employer–employee relations were paternalistic, he was seen as both a community benefactor and a respected employer. Among the industrial titans of his day, he was recognized as an innovator. He was one of the first to use electrical power in his factories (1883), the first to use the bisulphate process to produce pulp (1889), and the first to transport goods by truck (1905). Throughout his business career Eddy kept an eye on what was happening in the world around him and in his business operations. He was careful to accumulate capital to expand his operations and was open to new ventures in promising fields.

The terms of his will empowered him to keep a measure of control even after his death. The main beneficiaries, his partners, were to carry on his work for 10 years. Then, the company shares would be redistributed in favour of his second wife, who had to give up her claim to the joint estate in order to gain title to them. While the E.B. Eddy Company began as a family business, it no longer was one. Eddy's direct descendants, his daughter Ella Clarissa and his grandson Ezra Butler Bessey (who changed his name to Ezra Butler Eddy in 1912), were almost excluded from the estate. In 1896, in a precedent-setting legal case, Eddy and his daughter had gone to court over the inheritance left to her by his first wife in 1893. Control of the company, as well as considerable goods and property, went to the second Mrs. Eddy. On her death in 1921, control was handed over to her brother. And on his death in 1926, a friend and legal representative of the Shirreff family became the principal shareholder in the E.B. Eddy Company.

The E.B. Eddy Company continued to prosper after its founder's death. In 1927, the match factory was sold to a British corporation, and in 1943, a Canadian by the name of Williard Garfield Weston bought controlling interest. The E.B. Eddy Company acquired J.R. Booth's fine paper mill after World War II. Weston, subsequently, bought out the shares of that amalgamated company creating George Weston Limited, a consumer goods conglomerate that still exists today. Eddy's sulphite pulp mill and 44 acres of nearby property were bought by the government to be used as public parkland — a much more environmentally friendly option than lumberyards and pulp mills.

Ezra Eddy was influential in the Hull area and served six terms as mayor of the former City of Hull as well as his ten years as an alderman. Today, E.B. Eddy products are shipped around the world. The name can be seen on products from fine papers to White Swan toilet tissue. For 100 years after its incorporation, the historic E.B. Eddy Company was the largest employer and the largest industry in Hull (Gatineau).

Chapter 8
Thomas Ahearn
(1855 – 1938)

"The Santa Claus Trolley of 1896 toured around downtown on Christmas Eve with one of the electricity men of Ottawa seated on the roof tossing candies and oranges to the assembled onlookers of children and adults."
The *Ottawa Journal*, 1896

n 1885, electricity came to Ottawa. The man who brought it was called "the Edison of Canada." From telephones and electric lighting to streetcars and household appliances, Thomas Ahearn was a multi-talented Ottawa inventor and entrepreneur.

As a 15-year-old boy, Ahearn was so excited by the new technology of telephony that he went from his Le Breton Flats home in Ottawa to the J.R. Booth Company offices to offer his services for free in exchange for the chance to learn

Thomas Ahearn, circa 1903

about telephony. After becoming an expert telegrapher, he was ready for more challenges. Showing a great deal of initiative, young Ahearn approached the Montreal Telegraph Company branch office in Ottawa and offered to deliver messages (again for free) in exchange for a chance to learn more about the telegraph. Within six months, he was made an operator-messenger and paid eight dollars a month. In 1878, he took charge of the Ottawa Branch of the Montreal Telegraph Company and two years later, after spending some time with the Western Union Telegraph Company in New York City, Thomas Ahearn became the local manager of the Bell Telephone Company back in Ottawa.

In his next position, Ahearn was employed as an inspector for the Canadian Pacific Railway (CPR) Telegraph System. He later worked in the House of Commons telegraph office, where he made friends with members of Parliament and journalists in the Press Gallery. These political and media contacts would prove useful throughout his career in gaining him access to the top levels of government, as well as providing him with links to the press. Contacts from both groups also helped him to proceed with and promote his inventions. Ahearn became extremely knowledgeable about the electrical aspects of telegraphy, gaining the nickname "Electricity Ahearn."

Unlike the pioneer settlers, lumber barons, business entrepreneurs, and city developers of early Ottawa, Ahearn did not owe his status to building factories, mills, and waterways. He simply devised the power that ran them, the light that illuminated them, the telephone lines that connected them, and the transportation vehicles that allowed workers to get to and from them. He didn't cut down trees. Instead, he put up power poles made from them. He didn't connect communities by canal. He connected them by wire. He didn't create a settlement in the woods. But he did make the settlement a better place in which to live.

In 1877, Ahearn invented a rudimentary telephone system based on an article he had read about Alexander Graham Bell in *Scientific American.* He took two homemade wooden cigar boxes, some magnets, and a wire, and, using existing telegraph lines, made a connection from Pembroke to Ottawa. With these simple tools, Ahearn made history; it was Ottawa's first long-distance telephone call. For his efforts, he was threatened with legal action for the unauthorized use of Bell's patent. However, it was this sort of impressive talent that prompted the Bell Telephone Company to make him manager of their first Ottawa office. He later sold the cigar boxes to settle a $16 hotel bill.

Following his famous long-distance telephone call, Ahearn teamed up with Warren Soper to open a store on Sparks Street. Soper was born in Maine but, as a young child, moved to Ottawa with his family. The two men first met through their common interests. Each became an expert telegraph operator and their careers brought them together. While neither man was a shrinking violet when it came to business opportunities, Ahearn was usually the front man while Soper took care of things behind the scenes. This helped them to avoid what could have been a monumental clash of egos. It also allowed them to create a partnership to conduct electrical engineering and contracting.

Ahearn and Soper Electrical Contractors was formed in 1882, with Thomas Ahearn as president and Warren Soper as vice-president. The partners then proceeded to create one innovative company after another in the fields of light, heat, power, and transportation. In addition, they became representatives for the Westinghouse Electrical Manufacturing Company of Chicago. At the same time, they were building long-distance telephone lines to Pembroke, Montreal, and Quebec City for the Bell Telephone Company.

In 1884, Ahearn married Lilias Mackey of Ottawa. They had two children, a son and a daughter, whom they named after themselves. Thomas Franklin Ahearn later became a member of Parliament and president of Rowatt–Ahearn Limited, insurance brokers. Lilias married H.S. Southam, a prominent newspaper publisher. She also had a career, as headmistress of Elmwood School (an independent educational institution for young women).

Throughout his lifetime, Ahearn was a prominent Liberal and later in life was appointed by the prime minister to head a new Federal District Commission (the forerunner of today's National Capital Commission). During this time, Ahearn was instrumental in assembling the land for Confederation Square in downtown Ottawa.

By 1885, Ahearn and Soper, who were now co-owners of the Ottawa Electric Company (OEC), installed 165 arc street-lamps and electrified Ottawa. The arc lamp was the first development in electric lighting. The original gas lights cast a pale yellow glow in houses and on street corners. The carbon-arc lamp was a device in which an electric current zapped across a gap between two carbon rods and formed a bright discharge called an arc. The new technology spread quickly, and the arc lamps were widely used in cities. Early lamps of this type were made with an open arc. But later ones were enclosed in glass, and were therefore much more practical. The glass globe kept out rain, snow, and gusts of wind that could otherwise extinguish the light.

Suddenly, people could have electric bulbs to illuminate their homes and electric streetlights to light up the night. The power business was an immediate success throughout Canada. Many different companies, in addition to Ahearn and Soper, were formed to provide electric power to consumers in other cities and provinces. Competition was fierce and small companies amalgamated to form bigger ones. Unfortunately, rates were high and service was poor.

There was also discomfort among residents about the effects of "turning night into day." The light was "brilliant enough ... but the difficulty in its efficient working appears to be ample steady power for driving the dynamo machine," observed the local newspaper, the *Journal.* City council was also not fully supportive of the light business. There was the possibility of profit, but there was also the risk of losing public monies on flighty new inventions, not to mention a firm attachment to the status quo. "In short," said Mayor C.H. Mackintosh in an 1891 report, "day light has been such a cheap blessing hitherto that the payment of $150,000 per annum for a little more of it, will scarcely meet with the approbation of those who take a practical view of the subject."

By 1901, one of Ahearn and Soper's private companies, Ottawa Electric Company, had bought up all the smaller companies and enjoyed a monopoly in the Ottawa market — in spite of Ottawa City Council entering into the fray and creating competition by funding the Consumer Electric Company. The OEC merged with the Ottawa Gas Company to form the Ottawa Light, Heat, and Power Company (OLHPC). For the next 40 years, the OLHPC fought an ongoing battle with its city-sponsored rival. Finally, the city-funded company bought out Ahearn and Soper's company, paying $7.6 million for two generating stations at the Chaudière Falls and 35,797 customer accounts.

Thomas Ahearn made his reputation, and his money, in electricity. But electricity was one of the few products that showed a price decrease over time. In 1905, the residential electricity rate was eight cents per kilowatt hour (kWh) plus one dollar a year to rent the metre. By 1968, the bimonthly rate was two cents per kWh for the first 120 kWh, decreasing as more power was used. In 1968, the average household got a bill every two months for $13 ($78 per year). In comparison, the average 1905 telephone bill was $25 a year and in 1968 it was $63 a year ($5.30 a month). For most of today's consumers this would be a bargain, but it was a considerable sum in the early 20th century. And monopolies, not competition, were the norm.

Back in 1892, the Ottawa Electric Street Railway Company had constructed a new electrical power station to harness the hydropower from the Chaudière Falls. A 400-horsepower generator, weighing 33,000 pounds, was purchased in the United States and installed. The *Ottawa Citizen* reported that this was the first building in the world to be heated entirely by electric power. This engineering achievement consisted of water pipes running through brick-lined conduits beneath the floor. The water in the pipes was heated by an electrical apparatus invented by none other than Thomas Ahearn.

Not content to keep streets alight, buildings heated, and people warm, Ahearn turned his inventive mind to cooking food on an electric stove. His achievement was celebrated at the Windsor Hotel in Ottawa, where a select group of guests were invited to sit down to an "electric dinner," one cooked entirely by electricity. On August 29, 1892, Ahearn was celebrated as the first person in the world to use a device to cook food with electricity. His workshop served as the kitchen for the banquet, which featured a menu of Saginaw Trout with Potato Croquettes, Sauce Tartare, and Strawberry Puffs. The *Ottawa Journal* called it "cooking by the agency of chained lightning."

However, the introduction of electric labour-saving devices such as washing machines, sewing machines, and cooking appliances was not always well received by the public. People were, in general, suspicious of "new-fangled" contraptions. At least one Canadian preacher took to his pulpit and went on record to criticize the new devices as "an invention of the devil [that] would relieve girls from honest toil to wander about the streets and fall prey to the wiles of Satan."

In 1893, Ahearn and Soper were given the contract to light up the Parliament Buildings with thousands of electric lights for Queen Victoria's Diamond Jubilee in 1897. They also took their electric light show to the streets. On Christmas Eve, the pair decorated a streetcar with electric lights and each took a shift, dressed as Santa Claus, to throw candy, nuts, apples, and oranges to the crowds of children who followed along behind the car.

While steam-driven railways crossed the countryside, the idea of using urban trains by running rail lines down the middle of city streets was just being developed. Before electrification, horse-drawn trams were the norm. They were used in New York City until electric trains were put into service in 1881. But the electric streetcar was not seriously considered as regular transportation in Ottawa because of severe winter weather in the capital. Undeterred, Ahearn and

Soper set up the Ottawa Electric Railway Company in 1891. Ahearn's son Frank, then a boy of five, closed the switch to start the first service. Ahearn then drove the first tramcar out onto the roadway. Frank was later to become the president of the Ottawa Electric Railway Company on the passing of his father.

In the summer of 1891, thousands of spectators gathered along the route from the streetcar garages in the Albert Street industrial district near the base of Parliament Hill to the exhibition grounds at Lansdowne Park. President Thomas Ahearn was the motorman of the first of four open cars. Numbers 10, 11, 12, and 13, packed with guests for the free run, formed a leisurely procession to the enthusiastic cheers of onlookers on both sides of the street. At the end of the inaugural trip, an outdoor luncheon was served amid lavish decorations. According to one reporter, "thousands lined the route to view the strange sight of cars that ran without being pulled or pushed while horses frantically tried to get away from their drivers."

But winter operations were a problem. When snow filled in the tracks the cars did not work. People froze sitting in the cold cars. It was just as cold to ride as it was to walk. The snow problem threatened to prevent the winter use of streetcars. Ahearn gave this issue some thought and came up with a solution. He manufactured a specially designed electric sweeper in the form of an enormous cylindrical broom which rotated at high speed in front of the car. It created a

Ottawa Electric Railway Car #65, circa 1897

cloud of snow and ice as it cleared the track over which the streetcar would immediately travel. However, the city then demanded that the company remove the snow from any street on which it had streetcar lines. This demand was also addressed. The problem was eliminated by loading the snow onto horse-drawn snow-box sleighs. The sleighs cleared the snow off the streets. And of course the sleighs, the horses, and the men just happened to work for Ahearn and Soper.

Not stopping there, Ahearn next tackled the problem of cold by creating the first heated cars in North America. He warmed the cars by running electrically heated water under the floors, much as he had done at the Chaudière Falls power station. If passengers found this apparatus to be of dubious safety, they had only to recall that it replaced an onboard wood stove that necessitated straw on the streetcar floor. And it was the streetcar that changed the design of cities. No longer did workers have to live within walking distance of their jobs. Take the streetcar and your residence could be anywhere near a tramline. Cities developed suburbs and people not only took streetcars to work, but also to parks and amusement centres on their days off. Ahearn was again ahead of his time when he argued before city council for (and was allowed to run) a Sunday tram service in 1900. There was great opposition from religious and other groups because many people believed that the Sabbath Day, the poor man's day, would be ruined by immorality.

Ottawa's first 10 streetcars were purchased in St. Catharines, Ontario, and were finished in polished oak. But soon they were being built locally to Ahearn and Soper specifications. This was the Ottawa Car Company (OCC) component of their multi-business conglomerate. The OCC designed, built, and repaired streetcars and associated equipment in the company's plant. As the tramlines grew out into the suburbs, the Ottawa Car Company also grew. During the commute, passengers could sit on red plush seats with their toes toasty warm thanks to the inventive Thomas Ahearn. These were the first electrically heated tramcars on the continent. An article in *Canadian Engineer* commented: "In no city in the Temperate Zone is street railway traffic so comfortable. On the coldest day in winter the seats are as comfortable as on the balmiest day in summer, every car being heated by electricity, and kept at uniform temperature."

The ongoing operations of Soper and Ahearn were largely directed — with great attention to detail — from the head offices of the company on Sparks Street by means of notes and phone calls from the two owners to James E. Hutchison, their the first superintendent. He worked out of the Ottawa Electric Railway office on Albert Street. When a car passed the Sparks Street office with a problem, such as a flat wheel, a loud voice would yell, "Get the number of that car!" An employee would look out the window and yell back, "Number 26, sir." An immediate telephone call to Hutchison on Albert Street would follow with the order, "Jim, car 26 just passed here with a flat wheel ... take it off." And car 26 went off for repairs.

Prime Minister Mackenzie King appointed Thomas Ahearn chairman of the Broadcasting Committee for the 1917 Diamond Jubilee of Confederation. Ahearn's task was to produce a coast-to-coast radio broadcast of the festivities on Parliament Hill, a job that required the stringing of 32,000 kilometres of wire. On the ground, Ahearn was responsible for developing much of the city's parkway system. He once said that his one ambition was "to see the Capital of Canada become the greatest and most beautiful city on the continent." This ambition was finally within his grasp.

Well-connected politically, he was appointed by the prime minister to head the new Federal District Commission which assembled the land for Confederation Square in the heart of Ottawa. This powerful commission effectively replaced municipal control with federal jurisdiction.

Thomas Ahearn was the first Ottawa millionaire to make his fortune outside of the lumber business. At the time of his death in 1938, he was a utilities titan who had been the president of nine major firms and the holder of six director-ships. In addition, Ahearn had a seat on the Privy Council, was the chairman of two key public offices, and the patent-holder of 11 Canadian inventions.

Today, every time people in Ottawa turn on a light, an electric heater, or the water taps, every time they use a stove or an electric iron, pick up the phone, or take a bus, they are beholden to the man who went from being a telegrapher to being a leader in Ottawa utilities and finance.

Epilogue

While this is not a comprehensive accounting of all the people who contributed to the development of Canada's National Capital Region, it does give one an idea of the personal qualities that were necessary for success in settling a new land and in developing new technologies. The capital titans started small and grew big. Was there a rivalry among them? Yes, of course. They jostled each other to acquire land, to build mills, transportation systems, and communities. But, when the need arose, they also co-operated for their mutual benefit. Not all their joint ventures were successful. And some of their relationships were downright acrimonious.

Ottawa began as a small encampment in the wilderness. Its survival depended on mutual respect and tolerance. Although overlapping in areas and in times, each of the titans had their own individual spheres of influence. Philemon Wright built a community on agriculture and timber. John By built a canal linking two commercial centres. Thomas MacKay built enduring works in stone. Nicholas Sparks built the city centre. And the three lumber barons — John Egan, J.R. Booth, and E.B. Eddy — built the industrial base for the capital. Thomas Ahearn, least known of the titans, built the electrical, transportation, and communications base that tied Ottawa's people and businesses together.

Bibliography

Andrews, Mark E. *For King and Country: Lieutenant Colonel John By R.E., Indefatigable Civil–Military Engineer.* Merrickville, Ontario: The Heritage Merrickville Foundation, 1998.

Edgar, J.D. *Canada and Its Capital: with Sketches of Political and Social Life at Ottawa.* Toronto: Morang, 1898.

Haig, Robert. *Ottawa, City of the Big Ears.* Ottawa: Haig and Haig Publishing Co., 1969.

Legget, Robert F. *Rideau Waterway.* Toronto: University of Toronto Press, 1986.

Lett, William Pittman. *Reflections of Bytown and its old Inhabitants.* Ottawa: Citizens Printing and Publishing Company, 1874.

Mika, Nick and Helma. *Bytown, the Early Days of Ottawa.* Belleville, Ontario: Mika Publishing Company, 1982.

Negru, John. *The Electric Century; an illustrated history of electricity in Canada.* Montreal: The Canadian Electrical Association, 1990.

Ross, A.H.D. *Ottawa Past and Present.* Toronto: Musson Book Company, 1927.

Taylor, John A. *Ottawa: An Illustrated History.* Toronto: James Lorimer & Company and Canadian Museum of Civilization, 1986.

Trinnell, John Ross. *J.R. Booth: the Life and Times of an Ottawa Lumberking.* Ottawa: Treehouse Publishing, 1998.

Woods, Shirley E. Jr. *Ottawa, The Capital of Canada*, Toronto: Doubleday Canada Limited, 1980.

Wright Carr-Harris, Bertha. *The White Chief of the Ottawa* Toronto: William Briggs, 1903.

Acknowledgments

No work is ever created in isolation. There are many inputs, influences, experiences, and events that flavour a finished product. This is also true of *Ottawa Titans*. It is the product of its creative environment.

Living in Ottawa with ready access to the National Archives of Canada (NAC) and the University of Ottawa Library makes life easier for any researcher and writer. The search for material in this book was facilitated by access to their holdings. And, being a member of a national organization like the Periodical Writers Association of Canada (PWAC) is a boon to any working writer. The discussions and encouragement contribute to getting the job done.

Naturally, choosing well in choosing a partner makes life much more pleasant. I chose well in Bob Mercier. To you, Bob!

About the Author

L. D. Cross is an Ottawa writer and member of the Periodical Writers Association of Canada (PWAC). Her business and lifestyle articles have appeared in publications such as *Home Business Report, Modern Woman, WeddingBells, Fifty-Five Plus, enRoute, Aviation History,* and *Legion Magazine.* She has won awards of excellence for features and for editorial and technical writing in the International Association of Business Communicators (IABC) Ottawa *EXCEL* competitions.

Cross is also co-author of *Inside Outside: In Conversation with a Doctor and a Clothing Designer,* which is about achieving a lifetime of feeling good and looking good.

Photo Credits

All images from **National Archives of Canada**: front cover photograph by William James Topley (PA-008440); pg. 18 painting by unknown artist (C-011056), pg. 31 painting by Charles W. Jefferys, 1869-1951 (C-73703), pg. 38 (C-28531), pg. 55 (C-002846), pg. 71 (PA-008405), pg. 87 lithograph by Edwin Whitfield (C-000600), pg. 93 photograph by William James Topley (PA-28001), pg. 108 photograph by William James Topley (PA-026419), pg. 111 (C-121146), pg. 120 photograph by William James Topley (PA-012222), pg. 127 (PA-1366697).

AMAZING STORIES
NOW AVAILABLE!

AMAZING STORIES™

ALBERTA TITANS

From Rags to Riches During
Alberta's Pioneer Days

BUSINESS/BIOGRAPHY
by Susan Warrender

Alberta Titans
ISBN 1-55153-983-7

AMAZING STORIES

NOW AVAILABLE!

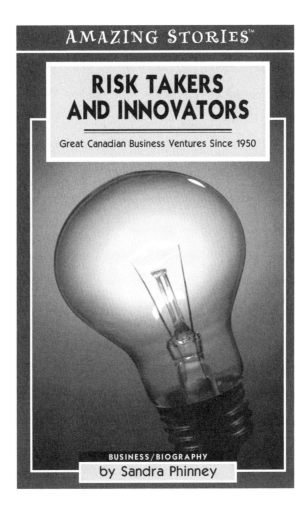

AMAZING STORIES™

RISK TAKERS AND INNOVATORS

Great Canadian Business Ventures Since 1950

BUSINESS/BIOGRAPHY
by Sandra Phinney

Risk Takers and Innovators
ISBN 1-55153-974-8

AMAZING STORIES
NOW AVAILABLE!

AMAZING STORIES™

STRANGE EVENTS

Incredible Canadian Monsters,
Curses, Ghosts, and Other Tales

MYSTERY/HISTORY
by Johanna Bertin

Strange Events
ISBN 1-55153-952-7

AMAZING STORIES
NOW AVAILABLE!

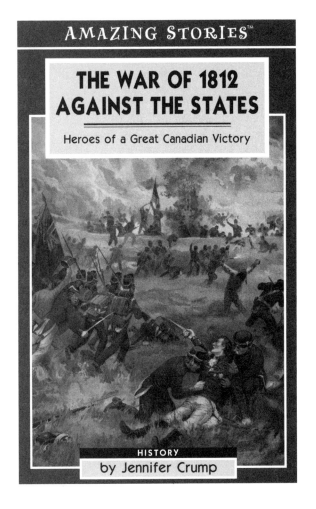

AMAZING STORIES™

THE WAR OF 1812 AGAINST THE STATES

Heroes of a Great Canadian Victory

HISTORY
by Jennifer Crump

The War of 1812 Against the States
ISBN 1-55153-948-9

AMAZING STORIES
NOW AVAILABLE!

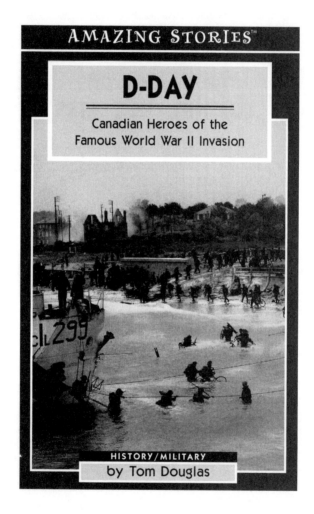

AMAZING STORIES™

D-DAY

Canadian Heroes of the
Famous World War II Invasion

HISTORY/MILITARY
by Tom Douglas

D-Day
ISBN 1-55153-795-8

AMAZING STORIES

NOW AVAILABLE!

AMAZING STORIES™

UNSUNG HEROES OF THE ROYAL CANADIAN AIR FORCE

Incredible Tales of Courage and
Daring During World War II

HISTORY

by Cynthia J. Faryon

Unsung Heroes of the Royal Canadian Air Force
ISBN 1-55153-977-2

OTHER AMAZING STORIES

ISBN	Title	Author
1-55153-983-7	Alberta Titans	Susan Warrender
1-55153-943-8	Black Donnellys	Nate Hendley
1-55153-966-7	Canadian Spies	Tom Douglas
1-55153-795-8	D-Day	Tom Douglas
1-55153-982-9	Dinosaur Hunters	Lisa Murphy-Lamb
1-55153-970-5	Early Voyageurs	Marie Savage
1-55153-996-9	Emily Carr	Cat Klerks
1-55153-968-3	Edwin Alonzo Boyd	Nate Hendley
1-55153-961-6	Étienne Brûlé	Gail Douglas
1-55153-973-X	Great Canadian Love Stories	Cheryl MacDonald
1-55153-946-2	Great Dog Stories	Roxanne Snopek
1-55153-958-6	Hudson's Bay Company Adventures	Elle Andra-Warner
1-55153-969-1	Klondike Joe Boyle	Stan Sauerwein
1-55153-967-5	Marie-Anne Lagimodiere	Irene Gordon
1-55153-964-0	Marilyn Bell	Patrick Tivy
1-55153-962-4	Niagara Daredevils	Cheryl MacDonald
1-55153-945-4	Pierre Elliott Trudeau	Stan Sauerwein
1-55153-981-0	Rattenbury	Stan Sauerwein
1-55153-991-8	Rebel Women	Linda Kupecek
1-55153-956-X	Robert Service	Elle Andra-Warner
1-55153-980-2	Legendary Show Jumpers	Debbie G-Arsenault
1-55153-997-7	Sam Steele	Holly Quan
1-55153-954-3	Snowmobile Adventures	Linda Aksomitis
1-55153-950-0	Tom Thomson	Jim Poling Sr.
1-55153-976-4	Trailblazing Sports Heroes	Joan Dixon
1-55153-977-2	Unsung Heroes of the RCAF	Cynthia Faryon
1-55153-989-6	Vancouver's Old-Time Scoundrels	Jill Foran
1-55153-987-X	Wilderness Tales	Peter Christensen
1-55153-948-9	War of 1812 Against the States	Jennifer Crump
1-55153-873-3	Women Explorers	Helen Y. Rolfe

These titles are available wherever you buy books. If you have trouble finding the book you want, call the Altitude order desk at 1-800-957-6888, e-mail your request to: orderdesk@altitudepublishing.com or visit our Web site at www.amazingstories.ca

New AMAZING STORIES titles are published every month. If you would like more information, e-mail your name and mailing address to: amazingstories@altitudepublishing.com.